CW00495776

Independent Thinking on wish I had early on in my t out, actions become habit effective habits early on ir for life. This book is full of neat 'hacks' to save time, such as sharing powerful and engaging morning routines and simple ways to hand over more responsibility to the children. A great guide to developing an effective, efficient classroom.

BECKY CARLZON, CLASSROOM PRACTITIONER AND CREATOR OF THE LEARNING PIONEERS COMMUNITY

It would appear that Mr Creasy is an incredibly real and down-to-earth guy, and that's exactly what the frantic world of education needs. Frankly, I wish I'd been armed with this book in my induction year – because I'd have been on top of the world on a daily basis! His advice, tips and strategies aren't fluffed up with a mountain of psychology; they just work. They 'do what they say on the tin'. And if that makes your life easier, then what's not to love?

STUART SPENDLOW, DEPUTY HEAD TEACHER AND CO-AUTHOR OF *THE ART OF BEING A BRILLIANT PRIMARY TEACHER*

This book is easy to read and is jam-packed with years and years' worth of wisdom from an experienced teacher. Mark's insights will generate thinking, reflection and action in teachers at every stage of their career. Early career teachers will pick up tons of strategies they can implement easily, while more experienced teachers will reflect on their own practice and consider how they can make it even better – and all will smile at Mark's understanding of how schools, their staff, their pupils and their parents work and behave.

Reading *Independent Thinking on Primary Teaching* is akin to having the privilege of being present in Mark's classroom, in planning meetings with him, reflecting with him in the staffroom after a day's teaching, and observing his interactions with parents, colleagues and children, with the added benefit of a running commentary about his decision-making at every turn. And throughout the book, Mark's passion for teaching and love for the children he teaches is writ large.

**RACHEL TOMLINSON, HEAD TEACHER,
BARROWFORD PRIMARY SCHOOL**

How I wish *Independent Thinking on Primary Teaching* had been on my shelf when I first started teaching. It would by now be falling apart due to constant use. Full of wisdom and common sense, this is a book of hope and possibilities in which Mark asks questions designed to help teachers consider the ways we work.

Each chapter encourages us to reflect positively on what we already know and do, and provokes us to examine this with optimism – enabling us to see there is always another way to look at things, and offering alternative strategies that may just make our lives easier and our environments for learning more effective. Mark is the kind of coach we all need in our classrooms: authentic, values-led and focused on creating the very best environments for learning – enabling us to work smarter, not harder.

**JULIA HANCOCK, DIRECTOR, BOUNDLESS LEARNING,
AND LEADERSHIP, LEARNING AND WELL-BEING COACH**

Independent Thinking on Primary Teaching is an early career teacher's dream come true, and will also be useful for teachers at any stage in their career who may want some practical tips and suggestions to reduce their everyday workload, in a smart way!

The author's practical advice builds upon best practices that teachers may already apply in their classrooms, or those that they simply need to refocus upon and adapt what they currently do. It is most definitely a teacher-friendly book that offers concrete strategies to help in everyday practice. It is an easy read that will also serve as a reference point for specific areas, such as marking and feedback, in which teachers may want to make changes.

**DONNA MARTIN, HEAD TEACHER,
ST MARY'S RC SCHOOL, ISLE OF MAN**

Independent Thinking on Primary Teaching is undoubt-ably essential reading for all early career teachers, but is equally useful for more experienced teachers who wish to reflect on their habits and discover new ways of working smarter, not harder.

The book is a really accessible read which is jam-packed with tips, advice and practical ideas in terms of establish-ing effective systems and routines, building strong relationships and focusing on what really matters in the classroom (and outside). Always keeping the child at the centre, Mark encourages readers to reflect and question why we do things the way we do – and reveals alternatives and suggests small changes to help us see that 'there is always another way'.

Each chapter focuses on a key area of primary practice and offers clear, structured and practical advice to support teachers to reflect and make considered changes in order to not only have a greater impact on outcomes for chil-dren, but also on their own workload and well-being. Mark's warmth and humour runs throughout the book, and the strategies and ideas suggested come from a real understanding of the pressures and rewards of teaching in the primary classroom.

**HELEN MARTIN, EXECUTIVE DIRECTOR,
GATEWAY ALLIANCE**

How rare to read a book on primary education quite so packed full of common sense and practical tips. Mark Creasy shines a spotlight not only on the nuts and bolts of learning, but also into the cracks of – or places between – those important aspects of school life that are rarely spoken of, or are swept under the carpet, but can eat up time.

And this book won't eat up your time; I read it cover to cover in a sitting (but with copious sticky notes on the pages I wanted to return to). I can see myself recommending it to teachers of all levels of experience. The provocative questions in each chapter will help any teacher or leader to anchor themselves back in the 'why' of daily practice, while the 'working smarter tips' are brilliant for dipping into, with lots of practical ideas to try.

Mark shares some inspired ideas about how to make 'learning breaks' multipurpose, but equally he is uncompromising in the expectation that teachers should know their children and their curriculum inside out, and tailor it to the needs of every individual.

**SARAH LEWIS, HEAD TEACHER,
ST MARY'S C OF E PRIMARY SCHOOL, OXTED**

INDEPENDENT
THINKING
ON ...

PRIMARY TEACHING

Mark Creasy

PRACTICAL STRATEGIES FOR
WORKING SMARTER, NOT HARDER

ındependent
thinking press

First published by

Independent Thinking Press
Crown Buildings, Bancyfelin, Carmarthen, Wales, SA33 5ND, UK
www.independentthinkingpress.com

and

Independent Thinking Press
PO Box 2223, Williston, VT 05495, USA
www.crownhousepublishing.com

Independent Thinking Press is an imprint of Crown House Publishing Ltd.

Edited by Ian Gilbert.

The Independent Thinking On ... series is typeset in Azote, Buckwheat TC Sans, Cormorant Garamond and Montserrat.

The Independent Thinking On ... series cover style was designed by Tania Willis www.taniawillis.com.

British Library Cataloguing-in-Publication Data
A catalogue entry for this book is available from the British Library.

Print ISBN 978-178135400-1
Mobi ISBN 978-178135402-5
ePub ISBN 978-178135403-2
ePDF ISBN 978-178135404-9

LCCN 2021949262

Printed and bound in the UK by
TJ Books, Padstow, Cornwall

For Jessica. You inspired everything in this book;
now I hope it inspires you in your career.

FOREWORD

As someone who spent much of his early life determined never to be a teacher, upon realising that it might be a career worth considering after all, I realised that I had a question to answer: primary or secondary?

My limited knowledge of either phase – that and forgetting what being a teenager entailed – meant I opted for secondary. I felt, naively, that I could have conversations with older children that I couldn't have with younger ones, and I wanted to be able to talk as well as teach, to connect and not just wipe noses. I have since learned, of course, that you can often have a better conversation with an excitable five-year-old than you can with a grumpy adolescent, and that a teenage boy can produce far worse than anything a Year 5 can, and so I often wonder what would have happened if I had gone down the primary route instead.

If I had seen Mark Creasy in action at that point in my dubious career planning – and he is one of those rare creatures who has successfully pursued both the secondary and the primary route – I might have been swayed to throw my PGCE hat into the primary ring. What I have observed in his work – which is also the reason why he is such an important part of the Independent Thinking family – is his ability to stretch children's thinking, learning and subsequent achievements far more than I would have thought possible. He gives children of all ages choices, options, freedoms, responsibilities, independence and the opportunity to shine on their terms, without ever letting go of what might be seen as the traditional values of standards, behaviour and high expectations for every child.

Mark's first book, *Unhomework*, is all about how you can make that whole homework situation so much better by not setting any. Not in the conventional 'Go and read this, write that, colour this in and memorise that for the test on Friday' way at least. The unhomework approach is about helping pupils create meaningful, personal, high-quality ('I know you're Year 5s but I want Year 6 level work from you') longer-term projects that are motivating and enjoyable for the children, comparatively painless for their parents and carers, and that hit all the necessary curriculum targets. In this way, Mark's approach has transformed primary life for so many children and their families. And if there was any test of the effectiveness of this approach, it was during the COVID-19 pandemic, with schools locked down but Mark's pupils easily making the shift to online and independent learning. After all, taking responsibility and learning independently is what they've always known with Mr Creasy.

It is this combination of standards, rigour, expectations and professionalism – combined with his creativity, risk taking, humour, love of children and willingness to do the groundwork necessary to then fully trust his pupils – that comes across loud and clear in this book too.

With the sort of practical common-sense suggestions that make you kick yourself and ask, 'Why didn't I think of that?!', Mark shares his proven strategies, tips and approaches to help busy teachers save time, energy, paper and ink, and enjoy a classroom full of motivated, happy, learning children. He even gives tips on how to get the best out of parents and colleagues too.

I don't regret my decision to opt for secondary rather than primary. Indeed, Independent Thinking came about thanks to the connections I made in my secondary school on the edge of Northampton all those years ago. I do know, however, that thinking about primary education as a one-way street that is all about the teaching rather than the interactions with the children was a rather shaky premise for making such a decision. Done well, as Mark Creasy shows, teaching primary-aged children is a wonderful two-way relationship, full of joy and surprises (and, admittedly, some dribbling), that doesn't have to rob you of your evenings and weekends either. If only I had known back then that there is always another way.

> **IAN GILBERT**
> **ROTTERDAM**

ACKNOWLEDGEMENTS

This book has been produced thanks to a cast of thousands – literally – as it derives from the support, encouragement and understanding of friends, family, colleagues and head teachers.

First, a huge thank you to my wife, Deryn, whose constant, unwavering support is my rock. She is the first port of call for many of the ideas in this book, which I then enact in every class, or the sounding board and critical ear for those moments of spontaneity I have had during the day when I've gone off-piste! Increasingly, over recent years, she has been joined by our daughter, Jessica, who gives me, sometimes unrequested, the pupils' view – something I'm used to, having taught her at the start of my primary teaching journey. However, I hope she realises that she has taught me far, far more than I think I've ever taught her and together with her mum they are my world.

Second, to my mum and dad, who sparked my interest in learning and thirst for 'being better' when I was a boy. It's never left me. You filled our house with books and inspiration that have served me a lifetime and I use this as the basis for my interactions every day. You're always there to listen to what I'm doing.

I also want to say a huge thank you to Andy Willis, someone whose friendship and sage advice I value immensely. Although not a teacher, as we coach swimming together, we get to spend hours at galas talking about learning and pedagogy, as well as solving all of the world's problems! This is invaluable to me. He is a sounding board and someone I respect and trust without equivocation, plus he provides something that every teacher needs: he gives me something outside of teaching to focus on – our swimmers!

Next, to my Independent Thinking and Crown House families, who have, again, made me believe that I have something worthwhile to say about education – particularly Ian Gilbert, who always makes me think anything is possible and has been taking a chance on me since 2013! Also, to Dave, Nina and Hywel, who always look out for me, and are always there to support me when I need it. And, at Crown House, to David, Beverley and Louise for making this book a reality.

To everyone in primary schools with whom I have worked, thanks for all the times you have 'gone with it' and those when you've just asked 'why?' I can't name everyone, but to those of you who know that there *is* another way and embody this daily in your actions, not just through platitudes and soundbites, I am so grateful that you have supported me – you know who you are!

And last, but most certainly not least, I cannot fail to acknowledge all the input of the children whom I have taught, and their parents. You are the reason why I do this job, why I still love my job after more than 25 years, and why every day I get up to see what exciting learning there is to be had. If it wasn't for all of you, this book wouldn't be possible, so a huge thank you to you for taking a risk daily and to your parents for giving me their trust in doing so.

CONTENTS

Foreword .... *i*

Acknowledgements .... *v*

First Thoughts 1

Chapter 1: Daily Routines **5**

   Why are routines important? 5

   Classroom expectations/non-negotiables 7

   The start of the day 19

   The settle 26

   The register and lunch orders 31

   Assemblies 33

   Seating and groups 35

   Getting attention (and failing to) 41

   Ending the school day 44

   Chapter contemplations 48

Chapter 2: In the Classroom **51**

   Planning 52

   Resources 66

   Marking and feedback 70

   That 'F' word again 77

   Chapter contemplations 80

Chapter 3: Learning Outside the Classroom **83**

   Playtime 84

   Lunchtime 92

   Unhomework 97

   Chapter contemplations 108

Chapter 4: Testing **111**

In-class assessment 111

Times tables 120

Standardised tests 127

Chapter contemplations 139

Chapter 5: Transition **141**

Annual transition 144

Key Stage 1 to Key Stage 2 transition 150

Secondary transition 153

Mid-year move *into* your class 157

Mid-year move *from* your class 160

Chapter contemplations 160

Chapter 6: Working with Adults **163**

Other teachers, especially your year group
partner 168

LSAs 174

MSAs 179

SLT 183

Chapter contemplations 192

**Chapter 7: A Miscellany of Smart Ways of
Working** **195**

Staff meetings 196

Display boards 203

Movement 214

Parents 216

Shows and performances 224

Chapter contemplations 227

CONTENTS

Final Thoughts 229

Appendix 1: Home Learning Exemplar *231*

    Daily tasks *231*

    Everyday learning *232*

    Extension activities – the Tudors *232*

Appendix 2: Working Smarter Transition Document .. *235*

Appendix 3: Minutes Exemplar *237*

List of Working Smarter Tips *239*

References and Further Reading *243*

FIRST THOUGHTS

I don't think that staff in schools, anywhere, have ever had to work harder or had more expected of them than they do now. Pre-pandemic, during the pandemic, and now, post-pandemic, the pressure keeps stacking up. This is a situation not helped by the fact that education is – as it has always been – a political football, which might explain why teachers so often feel as though they've been kicked around the park on a daily basis.

We're not going to change that, which means if we are looking to improve the way we work in the classroom to ease our workload, free up our evenings, improve the quality of pupils' outcomes for all the time and effort we put in and, who knows, even see something of a Sunday afternoon once in a while, we need to look to ourselves for help. And what better place to start than with a simple but very powerful question: why are you doing that?

Seriously, have you ever stopped and thought about that question? Just pause now and think about some of the things you do on a daily basis, the things that seem to define your working life. The things that mean that you spend most of your working week on the perennial hamster's wheel. Where did those practices come from? Why are things done that way and not another? Why are they even done at all?

Maybe you work the way you do because that is how it was demonstrated to you during your teacher training? Perhaps you picked up your methods during your first year as a teacher or from a mentor, if you were lucky enough to have one. Your methods worked that year, so why not continue? Or, alternatively, you could work the way you do because you have been told 'That's the way things are done around here.' Perhaps no one even said those words to you explicitly, but that was the message you picked up. Who knows, maybe you're even doing things the way you do because that's what you remember from when you were at primary school?

Actions become habits, and habits become reality if you don't question them. You lose the ability to even recognise that you have a choice in how things are done if you're not careful. Or, just maybe, you have never really reflected on why you work the way you do. But, as is becoming increasingly important in our high-pressure, high-stakes, top-down model of education, there is always another way.

That is what I am attempting to highlight in this book: to reveal alternatives, to show how things can be done differently in primary classrooms everywhere. Not a massive revolution, but so many little changes that add up to something better. Everything you read is based on my experience in the classroom – having taught across the primary age range in a wide variety of settings from tough estate schools to the independent sector – and I aim to highlight what you really can achieve when you tackle everyday matters with an 'other way' mindset.

I have tried to address what I see as the key elements for working in primary schools today, whatever your setting. Admittedly, I may have missed a few. It's a big job we do, after all. However, I have examined everyday practices and how the same – or even better – results can be achieved, not by *working harder*, as if that were possible, but by following the old adage of *working smarter*. To this end, throughout the book, I have included sets of working smarter tips which will act as a guide and a prompt to different ways of working. Alongside these, I have also included some questions, provocations and points of reflection. After all, I don't have all the answers and you will create even more alternative possibilities by thinking for yourself and reflecting on your own working practices.

Nothing I advocate here requires huge investments of time or money. Everything is also designed to help you reclaim your evenings and weekends, something more teachers need to do than is healthy for any profession. Too many teachers are way too close to breaking point, as evidenced by the perennial problems of recruitment and retention. If we take it on ourselves to revaluate our work and learn to be a whole lot smarter about it, this will surely help.

CHAPTER 1
DAILY ROUTINES

This is the first chapter, not only because for many of us routines are the first part of the day, but also because I believe that from these small acorns, great oaks really can grow. By 'routine' I am referring to all of the things that primary school teachers do on a daily basis that have little, or no, relation to teaching and learning: the administrative, bureaucratic, often whole-school elements of the day that no one ever seems to talk about during teacher training.

WHY ARE ROUTINES IMPORTANT?

Simply put, they provide structure and regularity for the teacher and the learners. Well-considered, organised and structured routines offer huge benefits to everyone as they provide certainty and clarity. The teacher and the learner can be certain that there are things that *have* to be done and that there are ways *in which* they have to be done.

When routines are flawed and haven't been properly considered, they become burdensome and time-consuming, getting in the way of learning. Any lack of clarity and consistency from the teacher leads to confusion for the learners, plus, for some, the opportunity to exploit the cracks for mischief and misdemeanours of their own.

If you want to see with your own eyes the power of effectively crafted routines, simply spend some time with your early years and foundation stage (EYFS) colleagues, especially during the self-directed learning elements of the children's day. Thanks to providing clear routines and responsibilities for the children, and having high expectations of them, the potential for chaos is averted and the room is, in fact, more akin to an orchestra playing a well-composed symphony or a ballet company performing a beautifully choreographed dance than the mad supermarket trolley dash many would envisage.

To achieve this carefully crafted performance there will have been thought, consideration and plenty of training, plus more than a few missteps along the way. However, in a short space of time, the EYFS teacher has the classroom working how they want it to. Ask yourself, if it can be done with the youngest members of the school, why not with the older ones?

Throughout this chapter I will explore those things that everyone has to navigate every day, including:

- The start of the day.

- How the children enter your classroom.

- How you meet and greet them and how they are settled.

- Taking the register and lunch orders.

- Getting to and from – and running – assemblies.

- Seating and groups.

- Getting your class' attention.

- The end of the school day.

These are activities that are usually part of your whole-school responsibilities or are determined by the head teacher. However, I will ask you to reconsider how you organise them in order to take ownership. Before I go through these daily routines, I think it is important to start with another set of behaviours which are common to every classroom; the benefits of getting them right are huge, but so many of us slip up when it comes to applying and sticking to them. Of course, I am talking about ...

CLASSROOM EXPECTATIONS/ NON-NEGOTIABLES

Unlike in secondary schools – where there's usually a set of predetermined school rules, often individually interpreted by each teacher a child meets on their timetable – primary schools do try to involve the children in the process of rule creation. We frequently see this as an exercise in democracy – I'll come back to this important notion later – and an opportunity to engage with the children so that we can refer back to the expectations, often with a flourish, as we remonstrate with the class, 'Come on, 3B – what did we all agree about this six months ago?'

These classroom expectations are usually created at the start of the year, including expectations for written and numerical work too, frequently in conversation with the children, and then printed, laminated and put up on the wall for all to see. I have even seen some teachers who get all the children to sign the list of agreed expectations, as some sort of contract. However, this in itself creates a problem, which I'll address shortly.

Ideally, when crafting this list, the children will come up with the ideas that you already had in your head and life will move on swimmingly. Unfortunately, this doesn't always happen. For example, in stating writing expectations, too many children in Key Stage 2 will still talk about

7

capital letters and full stops, which is a Key Stage 1 expectation. It may well be OK to include this as an expectation in the initial stages of their transition from Key Stage 1 into Key Stage 2 but it should certainly not be an expectation beyond this point. I would even advocate revisiting Year 3 expectations in January to remove that element and look ahead, rather than backwards. Another example is when crafting the expectations for working in maths. Teachers will be told that one digit per square should be an expectation in Key Stage 2, even though that's been in place ever since the children started working in books and shouldn't need restating.

When considering how you and your class create your shared expectations, what about ...

NOT STARTING WITH THE EXPECTATIONS ON THE FIRST DAY?

Instead, you could wait a week and then review what you have seen and discuss with the children what has worked and what has not. This will also allow the children to get a feel for how you want to run your classroom – never forget that it is *your* classroom. You are the adult, paid to lead it. I have always found that it helps to consider the classroom as more of a benevolent dictatorship than a democracy; the children have the power, as long as you let them.

PROVIDING THE CHILDREN WITH A LIST OF YOUR OPTIONS?

Rather than simply let the children choose their list, offer them a longlist first. This then can be whittled down to what all teachers have, which is an optimum number of ~~rules~~ expectations (for me it's seven).

Alternatively, you could use a 'self-pair-square' or 'snowball' idea to develop the expectations. This means that the children individually select their own preferences from the list, then agree these with a partner, before establishing the final selection in a group, after which you take responses from the groups. Or simply provide the children with the list and have a straightforward vote – this also involves less of a sense of personal defeat for the children as it is the teacher's ideas being voted on, not theirs.

I would also suggest that this approach works really well when used at the end of the first week. This way you get to highlight all of the positives that you have seen, and note the things that the children do automatically, so you don't need to waste time restating them.

START WITH THE EXPECTATIONS FROM THE PREVIOUS YEAR?

During your handover, why not carry over the expectations from the previous year and apply them from day one in your class? This brings with it familiarity for the children and it's hard to imagine any teacher will have previously established anything drastically different. Then, at some point within the first half term – personally I'd wait no more than a fortnight – review, edit and adapt them. Phrasing this exercise along the lines of, 'We've worked really well with these expectations, but they were for Year X; you're now Year Y, so are there any that you think we should change?' will help. Again, providing your own list of options to choose from, including the current expectations, will aid the process.

The bigger challenge, though, isn't so much how you come to a list of classroom expectations, it's sticking to them. These are, after all, your non-negotiables. And they are for everybody. For example, a common one, on every class' list up and down the country, would be along the lines of: 'We take it in turns to speak and listen to each other.' Which is all well and good in theory, but is it applied in practice? Moreover, is it applied rigorously and judiciously? Or, as is often the case, is this expectation referred to simply:

- When a discussion has got out of hand?

- When people have started shouting?

- When you're not being listened to?

- When it's 'that child'?

- When you've had enough of 'that child', but instead pick on someone else who is far easier to deal with?

WORKING SMARTER TIPS

MAKE EVERYONE ACCOUNTABLE

If you're going to have a list of expectations for your class, ensure that everyone, including the adults, is responsible for themselves, all of the time. That way *everyone* is held to account. Once you have created your expectations, it is everyone's job to adhere to them. True, early on in your relationships with a class there may need to be more frequent reminders, but within a short period of time everyone *knows* that these really are expectations and that they are to be maintained. Examples include:

- An expectation of not talking over each other. Challenge it *every* time.

- One digit per square. Get work rewritten to follow what's been agreed.

- Sentences need to start with a capital letter. Send away any child who hasn't done this so they can correct it for themselves. Do *not* do it for them. Do not even signpost it to them by indicating the error.

- You have agreed the 5Bs for thinking for themselves when they get stuck – book, brain, board, buddy, boss. Insist that the children follow it, and don't respond to questions until they do, especially when the task has been modelled or the answer is clearly displayed.

Ultimately, all this tough love pays off and your life becomes easier. In a short space of time your class works how you want them to, with the added benefit that any child who infrequently breaks an expectation is easily reminded, often by a peer, and serenity (plus your sanity) is quickly restored.

GIVE REAL RESPONSIBILITIES

Allied to making *everyone* responsible, all of the time, I would also advocate the idea of engendering the feeling that we are a team from day one. This can be done by ensuring any responsibilities dished out are real and never allocated simply as control mechanisms. You know the ones: 'Jane, you're line leader.'

Subtext: 'Jane, I can't trust you, so you'll walk next to me like a prisoner with the warden.'

Or: 'Jane, you're the line ender.'

Subtext: 'Jane, you're the class snitch, so go at the end and then tell me everything that happens.'

Either way, Jane and the class know the truth. Unfortunately, all too often and in a genuinely caring attempt to provide opportunities for everyone and create equanimity, class responsibilities are all about rotas, roles and monitors: collect the register, return the register, be the class library monitor, hand out the books, collect the books, etc. These, however, are not real responsibilities. Genuine responsibility is found in:

- Showing visitors around your classroom/school.

- Having a clearly defined role within the assembly crew.

- Having an elected role on the school council.

- Being the sports captain (*not* just getting a turn because it is rotated every match).

- Leading a warm-up.

- Providing feedback from your group, something which needs training and clear guidance.

- Presenting your home learning to the class.

When considering how much responsibility you give your class, what about ...

YOU DON'T ALLOCATE RESOURCES?

You could inform the children of the resources that are available to them, should they need them, and let them decide. Over time, this will need doing less as the children will make decisions for themselves. For example, bead strings and counting frames are kept in the same place every maths lesson, so the children know where they are should they need them.

YOU JUST MONITOR WHO ACCESSES THE RESOURCES?

You may feel the child does or does not need the resources, but how do *they* feel? Watch who takes them and then see what they do with them. I've seen plenty of children who like to have resources on their desk 'just in case'. True, you may have to prompt some children to pick a resource, but this is better done in a 'What could you use to help you?' way, rather than a 'You need this to complete today's work' way.

EVERYTHING DOESN'T ARRIVE FOR THEM PRE-CUT TO THE CORRECT SIZE?

Motor skill development is important, yet for expediency (and tidiness) it is often overlooked the further up the school the children progress. In the same way as you model everything else, why not model cutting skills and show the children *how* you want it done? Which, of course, brings us to the guillotine!

ALLOWING CHILDREN TO USE THE GUILLOTINE?

You could develop the skill of straight cutting and the joy of accuracy in using the guillotine, probably with some supervision, but why can't a child be allocated this task? It's possibly safer than a pair of scissors, plus builds in the responsibility of doing something for the whole class, rather than having 30(ish) children all doing it indepen-dently. This is also a great time to engage with a child with special educational needs and disabilities (SEND) (i.e. it's not just for the academically able child who needs some-thing to occupy them because they've finished the work), who can be talked through the sheet or resource as they are using the guillotine, thus combining pre-teaching support with responsibility.

YOU CONSIDER WHO MEASURES OUT THE PAINT?

For some reason, it is common that as children progress through the school this is done by the learning support assistant (LSA) or the class teacher, yet in most EYFS settings this will be done by the children. The expectations are clear and will be modelled – yes, mistakes will be made, and that's all part of the learning. What's more, surely as the children reach Key Stage 2, shouldn't we be *expecting* them to recognise what paint (or other resource, for that matter) they need? They can also learn how, if they have spare, to share with others.

In my experience, every one of these points is second nature to EYFS colleagues. Too often I have heard primary colleagues bemoan how secondary schools 'dumb down/baby/reduce' our Year 6 children who are well used to responsibility, but are we any different in our own setting?

So, what about organising some personal CPD with your own school's EYFS setting and discuss with your colleagues what they expect of their pupils? Most heads will happily provide cover for this, in my experience, especially as it's free training for you and will develop your practice too.

WORKING SMARTER TIPS

THINK BEFORE YOU SPEAK

I have found that having a set of stock phrases which you rely on and use *consistently* not only reassures the children, but also ensures that your message and expectations are clear for everyone. Over time, as we transition between subjects and breaks, I expect to see less need to use these phrases as the children know what's expected of them and eventually they are not needed at all as we naturally follow our everyday routine. However, they are always there to fall back upon as and when needed – especially after a holiday or on a windy day.

Here are some things that I say to ensure that, as a class, we get more done quicker, thus freeing up time to do more interesting things instead:

- 'Please can one person from each table get the glue sticks and someone else get the scissors?'

- 'One person from each table get the books, please.'

- 'Could you three hand out X, please?'

- 'I'd like you five to go and set the hall up for assembly, please.'

- 'As a table, get the books, scissors, glue sticks, pencils and pens away, and remember no one can do more than one thing.'

In doing this, I monitor who does what so that direction can be given if needed (there's always at least one who is used to not doing anything at home), plus I can see who volunteers for everything as an avoidance tactic or in a desperate attempt for attention and ensure that they don't always get the job.

One other point – I don't make it part of the expectation that the 'best behaved' or 'highest achieving' children get to do everything all the time. In my class, it's equitable and everyone has a chance to be involved. It's part of the collective responsibility.

MAKE SURE THE LEARNING DOESN'T STOP WHEN IT PAUSES

I believe that learning breaks are an important part of the school day; however, some colleagues often marvel at how I 'find time' for them. Yet, I am aware that some pupils do require movement breaks, or a change of sensory stimulus, so creating that opportunity for everyone is important. In fact, by following the tips in this book, I hope everyone can see how I find the time, especially as I consider *not* having them to be more detrimental and, ultimately, time-consuming.

For example, as I've shown above, setting up and clearing away is a natural, built-in way to provide a learning break for the class and to target those children who may need one most, without the need for them to leave the room. The evidence that it works is in the fact that I never have anyone complain 'But it's not mine' when asked to put anything away. We're all a team *and* we get more done this way.

During the restrictions imposed on us all as a result of the pandemic, with children being forced to sit in rows, the need for learning breaks and in-situ games were especially vital. I ended up teaching these to some of my colleagues. Exercises like '1–10 blast off' – where, without any prior communication or preparation, the children have to stand up one at a time in no set order and say the next number in the 1–10 sequence – are especially useful. The aim is to ensure that you can get to ten without two children standing up at the same time or a number being repeated. This also worked brilliantly as a topic development tool, with variations such as 'Name the planets blast off' or 'Name the Tudor monarchs and Henry VIII's wives blast off'. Both are very popular with my pupils, bringing a change to the proceedings, a welcome break and a much-needed injection of movement into a lesson, but without moving around the room.

The use of activities such as the ones that follow are ideal learning breaks for COVID-safe teaching and beyond, especially as most of them can be used to reinforce or activate curricular learning too.

So, what about ...

USING KIM'S GAME TO LEARN A TOPIC?

For example, you could show the children a picture of the solar system, then blank the screen, before showing the image again with one planet removed. This can be done repeatedly. Over time, as knowledge develops, remove the planets in order of size, mass, number of moons, distance from the sun, etc. This is a good way to check what the children have learned: can they spot the criteria you are using for removal?

Alternatively, why not show the children a fully labelled picture of a plant, then blank the screen, before showing it again with one label missing. Again, over time, this can be developed by swapping two labels, having more than one label missing or changing the picture of the plant. I have employed this great game for the 12 Greek gods of Olympus, the seven continents, the cities of Britain, religious symbols and more.

USING A BOOMERANG STICK FOR MORE THAN MATHS?

Many of us will use the boomerang stick (also known as a number stick) prodigiously in maths, but have you ever considered it for other subjects? For example, in history it is an ideal way to consider a chronology, the order of Henry VIII's wives, or the timeline of Tudor monarchs – even adding in the last Plantagenet (Richard III) and the first Stuart (James I) for good measure. Have you considered using a boomerang stick for the journey blood makes around the body? Or in teaching the stages of a specific skill in PE to ensure plenty of oral rehearsal before the practical?

USING 'I'M GOING TO MARS …' AS A LEARNING TOOL?

To play, you state, 'I'm going to Mars and I'm taking …' and you list something that fits a rule – for example, it could start with the first letter of your name, you could say the item with your arms crossed, or pause before naming the item. The key is that you *do not* reveal the rule before playing. Whatever the rule is, the children who follow it can also go to Mars! Yes, this game is great for memory and a nice one to play. But have you ever used it for learning? It's another great one for chronologies or lists, such as the Tudors or rivers of the world. For example, sit the children in a circle and you state, 'I am going to Mars and I am going to take my friend Henry with me', then the next child has to name another Tudor to take, which could be one of Henry VIII's wives, children or significant people like Thomas Cromwell. This is also great to play if you have a Henry in your class and they think it's them you have chosen! Alternatively, why not use it to develop the writing techniques you have been working on? Children can only 'join' the mission if they use – at your discretion – a simile, alliteration, an expanded noun phrase, assonance, a metaphor, a rhyme, etc.

I believe it is through having these clear expectations and fundamental elements of teaching in your toolbelt that you will be best prepared to tap into the power of routines to work smarter and find the gaps where time, effort and energy can be saved each and every day.

And where better to start each day than the day before? Let me explain ...

THE START OF THE DAY

WORKING SMARTER TIPS

'FAIL TO PREPARE, PREPARE TO FAIL'

It is vital to prepare for the coming day before you leave the night before. That way, should you get caught in traffic, fall ill, need to answer a parent's urgent email, get tied up for a bit longer in the staffroom or have to deal with any other manner of obstacles to your arriving in the classroom on time, your room is set up and ready to go. This also means that, should you unexpectedly be absent, the children will come in to find their classroom as they usually find it, all of which makes matters a lot easier for the colleague covering for you. What's more, if you have established routines effectively, as we've discussed, any colleagues who need to unexpectedly cover you will have a pleasant surprise as the children *know* what they are doing and will get on with it, unprompted.

So, if you've started the day the day before, how do you then start the day on the day?

Well, depending on your school context, the options are numerous. You can meet your class in the playground. You can meet them at the door to your classroom. Your pupils can enter en masse through a given entrance, or any other variation on a theme. And that's just your class. What about the rest of the children in school? For me, even if it is school policy that the LSAs do the greeting and marshalling each day, it is important that I get involved with the process at least once a week. Why? Well, the pay-offs are many:

- LSAs may be glad of you relieving them to get to their class in good time. They like to start the day in a clear manner too, but this is often sacrificed to ensure class teachers manage this. The LSAs have to come into the room later and hit the ground running.

- It will give your own LSA the opportunity to welcome the children into your classroom.

- You get to meet more children than just those in your class (especially important when you're new to a school).

- You become visible to all parents.

- You see how the children enter school and you can see more incidental moments. The goodbyes to parents or how a child walks into the school can be great indicators of emotions and mood that teachers can miss out on unless they are there to witness those moments.

What's more, when you do take a turn at the entrance, please actually *talk* to the children. I've been with colleagues who stand there mutely or, worse, simply chat to their colleagues as hundreds of children pass unnoticed under their wagging chins.

It's also a great way to hone the teacher's ultimate secret weapon – knowing children's names. Simply say hello to them all and ask their name. Add to this a comment about a hat, lunchbox, scooter, pair of shoes, school bag, headband or the likes and you've gone a long way towards building relationships and humanising yourself in the eyes of the children. Just be yourself in this situation. You're not trying to be their friend, but there's nothing wrong with being friendly. What's more, the more you do this, the more confident you will become and then children (and parents) will talk to you more too. Say to them, with sincerity, 'Have a good day' and the pay-off will be huge, for you and for them. In this way, no child enters unnoticed. What a great start to their day – and yours!

WORKING SMARTER TIPS

DO YOU SEE WHAT THEY SEE?

Stand at the door of your classroom, look in and ask yourself: what is this classroom saying?

Now ask yourself: what do you *want* the classroom to say to the children as they enter?

On a daily basis, I would recommend that the scene that greets the children is a calm and familiar one, something more likely to ensure a smooth and easy start to the day. Having music playing quietly in the background can help here too.

Once you are happy with what your classroom has to say from the outside, step inside and look at your desk from the perspective of a child in your class. What is it saying? I've often been amazed by how colleagues can insist on order and tidiness from the children (including one teacher who made marks on the tables to indicate where children were expected to put their equipment to 'reduce fiddling') and yet their own desk or workspace was usually in utter chaos.

Make sure your desk speaks for you, whatever it is you want it to say.

MEET THEM AND GREET THEM

Meeting your pupils at the door to your classroom is vital. Every morning I meet my class as they enter and shake their hands (or offer an air high five if COVID restrictions are in place), welcoming them into the room with a smile. It gives me the chance to look them in the eye and connect with each one. In this way, I treat them with respect, telling them – and showing them – that they are *all* important to me.

This greeting performs many functions: it's personal contact, it's a mature greeting, it shows each child that – irrespective of the previous day's events – today's a new day. I can have personal communication with every member of my class, and I can get an immediate sense of their mood. From taking this time each day I have been able to detect: upset children, angry children, hungry children, overexcited children and children who have clearly had a difficult start to the day or a problematic weekend. This means I can react as appropriate in all manner of ways, from finding them food because they have none to knowing I need to make time for them to chat about their cause of distress to finding them a clean uniform.

All too often, too many children can go unnoticed in a busy school. These are the RHINO children – Really Here In Name Only – something exacerbated when 'They're a Smith/Brown/Jones/from that estate/from that part of town/from that community, etc., so what do you expect?' Their authentic emotional state is only noticed by chance, or when there is some sort of disruption, or they act up. I'd rather try to catch any issues at the start of the day and aim to prevent them escalating, even if I can't solve the problem for the child.

And if you still have reservations about this approach, remember:

- No one is forced to shake hands; I simply say at the start of the year (or usually on transition day) what

I'd like to offer as a greeting and why it's important to me.

● It's no different to when the children collect certificates in assemblies.

● It only needs to be a simple handshake, up and down, with a 'Good morning, how are you today?' (Although I did once give my Year 3 class a choice of a handshake, fist bump, high five, wave, or just saying 'hello'. One child asked for all five, one created a special handshake just for him and me, and I have been spontaneously hugged by several boys.)

Ultimately, though, it's not really about the handshake; it's about how you set about connecting at an emotional level every day with every child in your class.

MAKE THE PARENT DROP-OFF WORK FOR YOU

For those colleagues teaching younger children, there is a fly in the ointment to this meet 'n' greet routine: what if they are brought to the classroom door by their parents?

In this situation, to ensure the day starts how *you* want it to, you have several choices:

● Set out your expectations about the importance of a good orderly start to each day at the beginning of a new term or, better yet, before the end of the preceding academic year (this is easier if your school has a 'year ahead' meeting). This will give you a point of reference to go back to if – more probably *when* – any parents start pushing the boundaries.

● Create some form of tag team arrangement with your LSA so the children are still greeted even if you become tied up with a parent. Even then, deal with them courteously but swiftly and remember that asking the parent to make contact via email so you can get on with greeting your class is not unacceptable.

● Have a drop-off point. I know many schools where younger children enter through an external door that leads to the playground, usefully passing through an outdoor learning area. Make the gate onto the playground the place beyond which is a no-go area for parents. You may need to station your LSA there so they can liaise with parents, but this does allow you to get on with meeting, greeting and settling the children at the classroom door.

● Borrow from the world of cricket. Batters, when deciding whether to run between wickets, use three calls: yes, no or wait. Be prepared to use this approach with the parents of your class and train your LSA in this too.

● Borrow from Tom Hanks. In the film *Saving Private Ryan*, Tom Hanks' character uses the line, 'Gripes go up, not down. Always up.' Don't think you have to deal with the parent just because their child is in your class. Perhaps they can be referred to a more senior member of staff instead or at least to the school office to make an appointment. Most schools will have a member of the senior leadership team (SLT) on hand at the beginning of the day, so make sure you use them well. They'll thank you for it!

THE SETTLE

When considering how your day starts, ask yourself:

- How worn out am I after just half an hour of my working day?

- How frequently is my class' lunch order incorrectly recorded?

- How easy is it for me to transition from the early morning activities into the rest of the day?

- What do I aim to get from the first 15–20 minutes of each day?

- What do I actually get from the first 15–20 minutes of each day?

- Do I support my learners to make the best start, so that they can give their best *every* day?

Just think – 20 minutes wasted every morning equates to approximately two whole days in just half a term, so over two weeks across the school year. It's even worse if this wastage is replicated throughout the day. But if you get these first few minutes right, everything changes.

What is the first thing the children do when they enter the room? Those early minutes, allowing for incidental conversations and catching up, are important for the children. However, once this is done and coats and bags are sorted, what happens next?

I would recommend that the tasks set here should be purposeful, not simply filler activities that allow too many children to try out their best avoidance tactics: wandering around to find a pen or pencil, 'just checking' with their partner, suddenly needing to refill their water bottle, rummaging through their bag like Mary Poppins looking for a standard lamp, etc.

WORKING SMARTER TIPS

START AS YOU MEAN TO GO ON

All in all, how you start the day sends an important message to the children. If it is a meandering and aimless opening to the day, with a hefty dose of chaos thrown in, there will be some children who will seize on that as enough reason not to be there at the start. After all, if school actually starts 20 minutes after everyone has entered the building, why get in earlier? It's like going to the cinema to catch the adverts. It also feeds into the 'My child never does anything in the last few days of term, so we've booked a holiday' argument nicely.

As an example, my class starts each day with 15–20 minutes of focused, targeted work. I tend to avoid reading as I have found that this promotes avoidance and not the pleasure element that I'd rather have associated with this important skill. So what else can the children do?

● Review the previous day's work or work from a bit further back (e.g. can they really remember how to add fractions?). This doesn't have to be in the form of a worksheet, although it can be. Instead, they could: write a report on the lesson, prepare a quiz on the main points, summarise the learning for an absent friend, write a postcard explaining the learning to a parent/friend/younger child, answer an extension question requiring them to apply the learning, create a poster detailing the main points, etc.

- Prepare the children for the learning to come later that day or that week, finding out what they already know. A table discussion accommodates the children's need to have social time, as long as they also have targeted work. An example would be my class discussing and recording answers to the question 'What makes a good father?' in preparation for our lesson about the story of Abraham.

- SATs preparation work. Yes, I know, I've said it! For me, far too much time is given over to this, so I prefer a little and often approach, using either a pre- or an over-teaching approach. I would vary the timing of this, so one day of the week doesn't become 'SATs day' and I also ensure that I refer to work we'll be doing later in the day to reinforce its purpose. For example, work on parentheses was introduced at the start of the day before the children were to write up an explanation about animal adaptations that they had already researched.

- Watch a video with the aim of being ready to discuss it or answer questions on it. I would certainly recommend the Explorify website for great science-related videos to engage children with a range of relevant topics.[1]

● Have newspapers out for the children to read or photocopies of front pages.

● Alternatively, as a free option, have *Newsround* playing from the CBBC website, which is updated at about 8 am each day.[2] This can become a great discussion point, in my experience.

● Another alternative would be to display a news headline and ask the children to decide what the story might be about, which can also be achieved by having pictures displayed around the room or on desks.

● Have some ICT time, especially if you can trick the children into learning! I've recently been recommended Prodigy Maths (a free site)[3] and now my pupils can't get enough of it, which means when they come in, they settle immediately at a computer.

● Display a Thunk for them to discuss (for more on this, see Chapter 5).

● Display an alternative thinking problem for them to discuss. Again, the Explorify website has great examples for science topics.

The important thing here, as I have highlighted earlier, is to have the room ready for the following day before you leave each evening so you really can hit the ground running each morning.

---

1   See https://explorifywellcome.ac.uk/.
2   See https://www.bbc.co.uk/newsround.
3   See https://www.prodigygame.com/main-en/.

Clearly, depending on the age you teach, how you organise this for your class will be different. You may choose to have instructions displayed on the board so your class can come in and get on with it, while you can be engaging with those who need support. Alternatively, you may want to leave a paper copy on each desk, making the work individual and differentiated for all the children. Furthermore, I would recommend that you do still ensure that books and any other resources are out, ready and waiting, to avoid pointless rummaging and searching. Overall, though, the children should come in and settle to something purposeful, something that doesn't need you to be leading it.

NEVER BE AFRAID OF THE DIFFERENT OR QUIRKY

One thing that I have found always engages my class is having an 'On this day ...' feature displayed. Although this can be used to extend the children's learning, it may not be linked to the curriculum at all. It can not only tie in with their interests or individual backgrounds but also your own – it is no coincidence that Elvis frequently features in my room! There are numerous websites to use for this, including Wikipedia's opening page, the BBC's 'On This Day' historic site,[4] plus numerous other similar anniversary-related websites.

---

4   See http://news.bbc.co.uk/onthisday.

THE REGISTER AND LUNCH ORDERS

These are both necessary (and legal) requirements; however, they can also take an inordinate amount of time to complete, get in the way of learning and (in some cases) give LSAs a ruse to avoid engaging with the children as they 'have to' circumnavigate the class to check on the food order.

However, when taking the register or food order is combined with a settle activity, the administrative tasks cease to take over. There's always another way when it comes to organising these tasks and you will find one that suits your needs as well as the school's. Ask yourself ...

CAN I GET A CHILD TO TAKE THE REGISTER?

You can check it afterwards but doing this allows you to circulate the room checking on the activities the children are undertaking. You also hand a genuine responsibility to a child. Additionally, you could ask the children to state their lunch choices when their name is called, with a second child recording each choice as the first calls the register.

COULD I GET A CHILD TO CIRCULATE THE ROOM AND TAKE THE LUNCH ORDERS?

I've used this with the 'wandering stars' in my class who tend to want to walk about anyway. It helps them get this out of their system and makes them feel positive, rather than being incessantly nagged to sit down.

WHY NOT HAVE THE LUNCH ORDER FORM GO AROUND THE ROOM FROM TABLE TO TABLE?

Again, this allows you to circulate and just monitor the order's progress around the room.

WHY NOT HAVE THE LUNCH ORDER ON A TABLE AT THE BACK AND THE CHILDREN RECORD IT THEMSELVES AS THEY ENTER?

You may need to try to avoid a queue forming here, but don't undermine this process by checking for any incomplete choices. Make the children do it. Make them responsible. An alternative is to have a large version (on your interactive whiteboard is ideal for younger children) for children to put their name/picture on as they enter so you can simply check and complete the order. Another variation on a theme is to have a printed register and the children can colour code their name (e.g. red = meat, green = vegetarian, etc.).

WHY NOT TRY NOT TAKING THE REGISTER?

Or, more specifically, not calling it out? If you've met the children at the door, then simply mark the register, checking that no one else has come in late (this is easier with set seats – see later in the chapter) and thereby not disrupting the settling activity you've set up.

These three elements of every school day – the meet and greet, the settle and the register/lunch order – are important but should not take over or disrupt. Done well, they help to establish your expectations about how the day will go. Remember the onus is on you, as the teacher, to get this right for the class. Organise yourself, provide clarity and purpose and I promise you it will happen for you – but *not* if it is left to chance. Make what you expect and what you accept inextricably linked.

ASSEMBLIES

Perhaps you are in a position, like schools in England, where there are certain, ahem, legal expectations as to what you should and should not do when it comes to assemblies. Maybe you are in a position, like schools in England, where you just do what you think is best and hope that nobody looks too closely.

Schools will have different approaches – SLT assembly, themed assembly, class assembly, teacher assembly, visitor assembly, singing assembly, reading assembly, prize-giving assembly and more – but I know for some people, staff as well as children, not to mention parents trying to put on a brave face, an assembly can be a test of endurance.

So, how do we not only survive assembly, but make it an important part of the school day?

WORKING SMARTER TIPS

SURVIVING ASSEMBLIES

Apply these tips within your school context:

● Know what time assembly starts and be on time. Not early – that's a rookie error.

- Get to know the routines. If your Year 6 class are always dismissed last, then try to arrive last, through the back of the hall, so the children aren't sitting there longer than necessary. Not only does this maximise working time in the classroom before you leave, but it also avoids them getting fidgety and being told off and reminded to 'set the example'.

- Get the children involved as the assembly crew. Could they organise the music, set up the hall, lead the assembly, etc.?

- Link the assembly to learning that will take place later that day, perhaps following it up back in the classroom with a quick circle time. This reinforces to the children the purpose of the assembly and the need to process it properly.

- Have work to return to after assembly, rather than starting from scratch when you get back in the room. This also means there's no time wasted clearing up *before* assembly.

- Have clear and simple procedures for getting to and from assembly that are manageable and without fuss. A simple 'Line up for assembly' instruction should suffice, with an equally clear 'Carry on with what you were doing' after the event. This also reinforces the idea that assembly is part of the school day, not an add-on (or an irritation).

Here are some other pointers that will stand you in good stead with children and colleagues alike:

- Smile. Look like you're enjoying yourself. It's amazing how many colleagues don't do this, even when children are presenting or being awarded. What's more, you might take delivering an assembly in your stride, but others may be terrified – so at least try to look reassuring.

- Attend. Don't send your LSA in your place just so you can have a coffee/photocopy/chat. Like a head teacher on an INSET day, being in the room where it happens sends an important message to everyone else.

- Don't talk. Model to the children what you're expecting from them. And definitely don't break your conversation to chastise a child for talking only to then continue yourself. I've seen this done in every school I've worked in. What do such actions tell children about status and power and democracy and equality?

SEATING AND GROUPS

Now I appreciate that this is a contentious topic, but my aim here is to try to get you working smarter and to make your life easier. Apart from control and, perhaps, name recognition (although surely that is more of a secondary 'I only see them once a week' argument?) when considering seating, ask yourself ...

- Why do I have set seats for all children all the time?

- Why does the seating arrangement in my classroom never change?

● Why does the seating arrangement in my classroom *only ever* look like this?

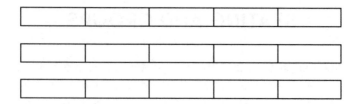

Note, I say 'only ever' like this. I love this configuration, certainly for group work, discussion, the ability to have a mix of children, allowing a 'snowball' development of ideas and allowing for the maximisation of space in my classroom. Many reasons. But it shouldn't be the *only* configuration.

Or maybe you can ask, do I have a classroom that *only ever* looks like this (and not just because of pandemic requirements)?

If your answer to any of the above is 'I don't/it doesn't', then great, but hopefully there are still things to think about in this section. If your response started with 'Because ...' then come with me and let's have a quiet chat.

Ultimately, what I am asking is whether you make the most of the seating arrangements in your class to make the children's learning better and your life easier. If you don't vary the arrangement – by which I don't mean simply allowing children to move seats – then perhaps not. So, when considering seating and groups, what about ...

HAVING 'BASE' OR 'HOME' SEATS?

This organisational tool works well for when the children enter the room (see 'The settle' on page 26). Not only does it ensure familiarity for the children, but it also makes checking absences far easier and creates a sense of belonging that I want my class to enjoy as I reinforce how important these tables are consistently, not just on day one.

If children are late, it's their home table's responsibility to support them in catching up with the task that has been set, avoiding disruption for the rest of the class and embarrassment for the latecomer. I ensure each table is mixed ability (and not just across maths and English), mixed gender and mixed interests, with a range of personalities, and I change these tables every half-term, without fail.

These tables can always be reverted to throughout the day, but they do provide a useful base for every post-break session as a way of reinforcing the recommencement of the learning. Furthermore, if the mix of learners is correct, it makes discussion work far more productive as there will be a range of opinions, which allows for better conversations to flow.

Do avoid the perhaps natural inclination to keep children sat at these all day, though. Yes, it may be more convenient for you – especially for control purposes – but the following mix provides a far richer flavour for learning. Beyond this, I would also suggest that it says a lot about your classroom culture and ethos.

ALLOWING RESTRICTED-CHOICE SEATING?

This can take a range of guises, but if you have created a sensitive environment and attitude within your classroom, all are applicable:

- Sit with anyone from your home table.

- Sit with someone of the opposite gender (this does require an equal split, I admit).

- Sit with someone of the same gender.

- Sit with someone you've not worked with this week.

- Sit with someone in your half of the room.

- Sit with someone in the opposite half of the room.

Whenever you allow choice, do monitor partnerships, but remember that when you allow the children to choose – in my experience – more often than not, they know what they need in a learning partner. In fact, just this week, when I gave my class a completely free choice, one of them asked me what the restriction was – they loved it when I said there wasn't one! However, there is also some guidance for this approach.

PROVIDING REAL CHOICES IN SEATING?

Simply put, let the children choose, with the caveat to 'make a good learning choice'. I would suggest making a decision about whether you introduce the task first, *before* telling the class that they can choose their partners, or let them pair up *and then* introduce the task – otherwise choosing partners takes precedence as you explain the task. My personal preference is to do the former, so the choice of partner is based on the task and they are less likely to simply pick a friend.

Here are a few pointers that may further support this process:

● Monitor who goes with whom. I encourage the children to work in different pairs, not always with the same people.

● Be prepared to (gently) challenge children about why they have paired together. I tell my class that they should be able to explain their choices, especially as I've asked them to make a good learning choice.

● Monitor who goes with the more able and watch out for any potential pressure on those children who some may see as able to do all the work while they (metaphorically) put their feet up.

● Be aware that some children may want to go in a three – if they can justify it and complete the work properly, why not? (*Teacher spits out tea while reading book.*)

● Monitor 'those children' who others may not naturally select for whatever reason – including those who sit, emperor-like, waiting for partners to come to them and then end up with no one, or certainly not the partner they'd want.

● Be flexible. Some children may want to work alone and that's OK too. (*Teacher spits out more tea.*)

USING RANDOMISED ALLOCATIONS?

There are huge amounts of these online – just search. Be prepared that you may end up with 'undesirable' pairings, but remember that these are learning opportunities too. If your environment and climate are correct, then it's always an opportunity for learning and the children may well surprise you.

By the way, don't create a randomised group only to regroup because of the allocations, or even because of children's complaints. Yes, there will be some winners and losers, but if the children understand why randomisation is done and, more importantly, the task itself is considered, everyone becomes involved.

ALLOWING THE CHILDREN NOT TO SIT, OR USING FLEXIBLE SEATING?

Yes, this is one for those teachers who are confident in their class, certainly not one for those who fear freedom and children's choice. Recently, I have seen people categorically state that sitting at desks – often in rows, but also in groups – is the only way for a classroom to be organised. My Independent Thinking colleague Jonathan Lear has written and spoken extensively about how flexible seating works on a daily and practical basis. I highly recommend his excellent book *Guerrilla Teaching*, in which he explains this in detail – or better yet, visit his school to see it in operation.[5]

This way of working is a great option for many children, meaning they can position themselves wherever and however they want. This may include:

● Standing.

● Laying down.

● Sitting on a beanbag.

● Working at a low table.

● Reversing seats so that they can sit backwards on the chair.

---

5 J. Lear, *Guerrilla Teaching: Revolutionary Tactics for Teachers on the Ground, in Real Classrooms, Working with Real Children, Trying to Make a Real Difference* (Carmarthen: Independent Thinking Press, 2015).

- Sitting on the floor using the chair as a table.

- Allowing the regrouping of desks as the children want.

However they choose to work, ensure that the basic standard, 'How you want to work must not impinge on how others want to work' is followed.

GETTING ATTENTION (AND FAILING TO)

Method 1 – 'Err, thank you … thank you … THANK YOU!'

Method 2 – 'Well done, Sanjay, you're sitting beautifully.'

Method 3 – 'Right, stop what you're doing … Paige, are you listening? No, pens down, right … everyone, Jana … right, now …'

These are just three ways in which we have all tried – and failed – to get attention.

Getting attention quickly and effectively is a vital tool in a teacher's box of tricks, but too often I find that colleagues across a school have such a variety of approaches that the children end up confused, noisily. While I do think that this is one for personal preference and will need variation depending on the task and when the children's attention is desired, to work smarter they need clear and consistent messages so that this is done with the minimal amount of fuss for maximum effect.

Before we look at how to get the children's attention, we need to ask a more fundamental question: do we actually need them to stop their work? And, even more controversially (so put your cup of tea down), do the children actually need to look at you? I have found that an inordinate amount of time can be wasted getting 30 pairs of eyes looking in one direction when it is not *always* strictly necessary. For example, if you have clear routines, then getting attention does not need to entail their eyes on you. Ears, yes, not eyes. (You can pick up your cuppa again now. You're safe, for a while.)

WORKING SMARTER TIPS

GETTING ATTENTION EASILY, WITHOUT THE BURDEN

What follows are a few suggestions for you to try out and experiment with, as well as some ideas about how you could use them to best effect. Ultimately, what you choose depends on you and what works for you with the least effort for the best results.

● The rain stick – my personal favourite because it's also so calming. Simply turn it over slowly and as the sound ebbs away from the stick, so the class noise should dissipate too. If needed, turn it over a second time, but point out 'That was twice; one too many times' and it shouldn't then happen again.

Best used: During individual or partner work, when there is a general hum around the room and you need everyone to listen, but not necessarily look at you, perhaps to explain the next stage of the learning or to introduce the extension/challenge work.

● Hand in the air – this *must* be accompanied with a confident stride into the front and centre of the classroom, standing still and silent. Be prepared for the fact that some children might not notice at first. Give them time. If you add a stereotypical 'I'm waiting' comment, they'll respond to this verbal cue, not the non-verbal one you're hoping to reinforce.

Best used: during silent/individual work, when you need everyone to look at you, perhaps to demonstrate or model something, or to share a child's work.

● Hand clapping – a simple three claps, to which the children respond with two claps and then everyone does one clap together. Or for the more adventurous use Queen's *We Will Rock You* opening riff. Just avoid singing the whole thing, if you can.

Best used: during partner or group work, when there's already a sense of collegiality and you want everyone to put their pens/pencils down (they can't join in the fun with a pen in their hand after all, can they!).

● Rhyme (and respond) – something like '1, 2, 3, eyes on me.' To which the children respond '1, 2, eyes on you.'

Best used: in the middle of an activity. I've found this one particularly useful during art for some reason. Painting by numbers, maybe.

● The bell – not the end-of-break bell, but an old-fashioned shop counter bell. You want it to be fairly high-pitched and rung three times spaced out, allowing everyone to recognise it and focus on you.

Best used: during discussion work.

- Pause/mute – I've used this just this year, based on a playground game my class played. The pause part is important so the children stop focusing on their work and can hear the instruction.

Best used: sparingly, but when a quick instruction/expectation is required. For example, 'Pause ... mute ... 30 seconds. By now you should have ... And I want to start seeing people ... Back you go, unpause ... unmute.' Of course, you can always try this without the unmute instruction. You'll be amazed at how many children stay muted!

ENDING THE SCHOOL DAY

'Oh. My. God. Is it home time already?! Come on, children. Quickly. Save yourselves. I'm old!'

I know many colleagues, of all levels of experience, who find that, somehow, the end of the day just runs away from them. To avoid this common mistake, when considering the end of the day, ask yourself ...

DO I KNOW WHEN THE DAY ACTUALLY ENDS?

I know this is simple, but it is amazing that some people seem to be oblivious to this fact – citing previous schools or changes in key stage, or seeming to think that it's merely a recommendation, as a reason. Once you are sure you know when the end of the day is, work *backwards* from this point.

DO I HAVE A CLEAR STRUCTURE FOR ENDING THE DAY?

If not, here's something that I find works for me – a simple five-step end-of-day routine:

1 Pack up.

2 Stand up.

3 Get your things.

4 Line up.

5 Walk out with me.

This allows my LSA to 'mop up' around the room, but it also works perfectly if they're not there to (or if I'm not there either, for that matter).

DO I HAVE A CLEAR ALLOTTED TIME FOR RETRIEVING COATS, BAGS, ETC.?

I believe you need to allow *no more* than five minutes before it's time to leave. It may require a little longer on a Friday when PE kit needs to go home, but it shouldn't.

DO I MAKE SURE THERE IS NO CRUSH AT THE PEGS/LOCKERS?

You can do this by dismissing children a group at a time with the clear expectation that this time is for collecting bags and coats, *not* chatting.

WHAT ARE MY EXPECTATIONS FOR THE CLASS TO CLEAR UP/PUT THINGS AWAY?

Again, make sure that there is time for this and ensure that the whole table is responsible for something. In this way, clearing up and getting bags can be part of your classroom routines. The alternative of you or your LSA doing it once the class has gone is not one I would advise. There are usually at least 30 of them and only two of you. Make it an expectation and part of your – and their – routine.

HOW CAN I EASE MY CLASS INTO THE END OF THE DAY?

I have witnessed teachers who create a 'Don't panic!' atmosphere by 3 pm because they've tried to cram as much work as possible into the day and the last five minutes become a rush to clear up and simultaneously get organised to go home. Of course, there will be occasions when this happens because we've got lost in the work, but the more we can do to avoid this chaotic end to the day, the better for everyone.

One way to achieve this is to end each day with a few minutes of story time, with you reading to the class. We know that far too many children aren't read to by an adult (according to a 2018 survey, only 30% get to enjoy this childhood activity[6]), so when you do this, it is a real treat (and especially rare if you are a male), as well as creating a calm end to the day. What's more, by ending on a cliffhanger – 'Find out what happens next tomorrow, children!' – you can set them up for the day ahead.

---

6 J. Peat, Only 30% of Parents Read Stories to Their Children Every Day, Poll Claims, *The Independent* (31 August 2018). Available at: https://www.independent.co.uk/life-style/health-and-families/parents-reading-children-books-uk-roald-dahl-mcdonalds-damian-hinds-a8516436.html?r=35964.

What else can I do to make the most of the time I have?

I know that many schools have PE in the afternoon, so why not send the children home in their PE kit? When they get changed for PE, tell them to put their uniform in their bag, leave their coat on the back of their chair and they are ready to go. This would be the continuation of what many schools have done post-lockdown, with children coming to school in PE kit on PE days, so why not simply maintain this process?

Alternatively, why not link the afternoon work with the early morning work (see 'The settle' on page 26). This means that work can be left out (*probably best if you put that cup of tea down to be honest*) – neatly piled so that cleaners can still see to the desks. This saves time and effort and helps children to see that learning doesn't happen in neat, composite boxes. Plus, I have found that coming in at the beginning of the day knowing that there's some interesting work to return to is a great lure for many children to get them in on time and settling quickly.

WORKING SMARTER TIPS

HANDING OUT LETTERS

'Oh, but Mark,' I hear you cry, 'what about when we have letters to give out at the end of the day?'

In my experience, this is a rarity, especially with email and other forms of communication that schools are using. However, I perceive that this issue is less about giving out letters and more about having letters delivered to the class mid-afternoon. In my experience, this is even more rare, but if it is commonplace in your school, speak to the office and explain how disruptive it can be. They possibly don't know or have been put under pressure to 'get these out before the children go home'.

However, if, like me, it is a rarity, having a clear and well-established end-of-day routine will mean it's easily absorbed. For example, simply give the letters out at the door as you dismiss the children so their parents see the letter straight away – not at the end of the week (or term) when the school bag gets emptied!

Alternatively, if your school is one where registers and letters are collected from a tray/box, why not just get the letters into bags straight after lunch, so that it's not a rush at the end of the day? Although, if you have a clear routine, as I suggest, it shouldn't be a rush, should it?

CHAPTER CONTEMPLATIONS

This chapter has been all about our daily routines. These are rarely mentioned, let alone considered, during teacher training. I am also aware that far too many colleagues never really stop to think about not only *what* they do every day, but – more importantly – *why* they do it so they can rethink *how* they do it (or even stop doing it altogether).

When considering your daily classroom routines, ask yourself:

● What are my classroom expectations and are my non-negotiables *really* non-negotiable?

- Do I make the most effective start to the day's learning?

- How much learning time is lost and what is the cumulative cost of this?

- Do I use the support of my colleagues to help me start the day well?

- How quickly does my class settle?

- What *real* responsibilities do my class have?

- How do I seat my class, and could I do something different?

- How effective am I at getting attention quickly without resorting to drill sergeant mode?

- What does the end of our day look like, and can I improve this?

- Can I work more effectively with my class' parents?

- Do I make the most of all the hands I have available to me?

And, for me, the most important consideration of all:

- Do my class arrive and depart excited about their day's learning?

Get your routines right and the answer to this will be an unequivocal 'Yes!'

CHAPTER 2
IN THE CLASSROOM

Whereas the previous chapter was all about getting children in and out of the classroom in a positive and productive way, this chapter is all about how to be better at what goes on in the classroom between the beginning and end of the day. In other words, your teaching and their learning.

Clearly, this is a huge field to try to cover, but I have distilled it down to what I perceive as the four key elements for success:

1 Effective planning.

2 The creation and use of resources to support learning.

3 Ensuring marking and feedback is effective yet not overly pervasive.

4 Incorporating fun into your class. (There, I've said it: the f-word!)

For each element I have looked at how we can make the most of the time we have to be as effective as possible, yet without anything becoming overly burdensome. Furthermore, I am maintaining my challenges to you that are the thread running throughout this book:

- What do you do?

- How do you do it?

- Why do you do it that way?

- How else *could* you do it?

And, of course, I will throw in a few provocations to help you consider and reconsider your practice. Ultimately, this chapter aims to give you some hope, especially if you are new to teaching, that things can be done just as effectively, if not more so, with less effort but some extra thought, consideration and strategic planning, and a desire to work that bit smarter.

Let's start with what seems to cause the most angst and concern, not to mention lost evenings and Sunday afternoons: planning lessons.

PLANNING

This can be the bane of many teachers' lives, but it doesn't have to be. Really. No, honestly!

I am all too aware that for many colleagues the stress around planning is derived from a variety of sources – the main one being wanting to do the very best for your class. This is a perfectly laudable ambition, and the advice in this chapter will support you in this. The challenge can be when this aim is coupled with an expectation (or even a demand) that you have to plan following the whole-school house style. Or worse, when the message is 'Do this because the inspectors need it'. In England, at least, this a myth, with Ofsted itself stating:

Ofsted will not:

- *advocate a particular method of planning (including lesson planning), teaching or assessment; it is up to schools to determine their practices and it is up to leadership teams to justify these on their own merits rather than by referring to this handbook*

Ofsted does not require schools to provide:

- *individual lesson plans*
- *previous lesson plans.*[1]

So now you know.

For me, the critical question is whether the style of planning you are using allows for bespoke and personalised learning opportunities for *your* class while also allowing *your* teaching style and personality to come through. If it doesn't, why do it that way?

First, though, a quick word of warning about those neat, expensive, off-the-rack, nicely packaged and marketed and very alluring curriculum packages doing the rounds currently. For me, they are full of false promises and will not ease your planning burden at all. Similarly, beware the 'Here's a memory stick with your lesson plans for the next term' approach that I'm seeing find its way into primary schools across the land. In both, the teacher's role has been relegated to 'delivering' the curriculum; the children's role to 'receiving' the curriculum.

I concede that a bit of a framework or route map can have its uses, but, ultimately, it is about *you* teaching *your* pupils in *your* community and in *your* context. No distant planning team (or even well-meaning subject lead) can achieve that in the way that you can. So, when it comes to planning – as with everything else we do – there's always another way!

---

1   Ofsted, *School Inspection Handbook* (1 October 2021). Available at: https://www.govuk/government/publications/school-inspection-handbook-eif.

WORKING SMARTER TIPS

MAKE THE MOST OF PLANNING, PREPARATION AND ASSESSMENT (PPA) TIME

(If you are a school leader, this tip is specifically for you!)

Joint PPA is a planning system applied in many schools. Is it one your school uses? If not, can you make it happen?

The concept of year team planning, which can take many forms, basically involves colleagues having simultaneous PPA. This is even better if the colleagues also have prescribed time each week for planning, but I know that this can be a step too far for many school leaders, especially with unavoidable absences and illnesses.

However, I think that joint/combined PPA is essential as it enables colleagues to meet, discuss and plan together for the coming set of lessons. Plus they can share resources and ideas for their classes – working independently together is a powerful free tool.

I would say to any school leader not utilising this approach, you are missing an important opportunity for supporting, as well as developing, your teachers.

So, if you are a school leader, ask yourself …

● Why don't we do it already?

● Why is our current system better?

- Do colleagues meet in their own time before and after school to give them the opportunity to plan together? (And, if so, are you happy about this?)

- Are there any logistical considerations that may prevent this being implemented? (For example, limited availability for cover staff.)

- When shall we start?

A word of caution, though, for teachers who do undergo joint PPA. While I fully endorse using joint PPA as a working smarter tool, I am aware that the division of labour can cause familiar problems. This is because, for the sake of expediency, colleagues will often divvy up planning in a 'You do the English; I'll do the maths' manner. This will mean that not only the planning but also all the resourcing for the set of lessons is completed by just one person.

While at the heart of this decision is the opportunity to allow the preferences and skills of all colleagues to be most effectively employed – whoever is 'better' at maths plans the numeracy, etc. – it becomes a self-defeating exercise and only repeats the issues I highlighted before, with the recipient still having to personalise lessons for their class. In fact, I have even worked with colleagues who created 'bland' lesson plans and resources, which they then had to personalise for their own class, thus creating double the workload for themselves!

When considering how to approach joint PPA as a teacher, ask yourself ...

HOW LONG HAVE WE GOT?

Knowing your time frame is important to ensure that you keep focused and make the most of the time you have. My suggestion would be to check where you each are against the year plan and then to get on with your class' planning for the coming week.

WHEN IS OUR PPA?

My advice here is similar to the previous point; however, note the disparity between being given 'a whole morning' and 'a whole afternoon'. The former is usually at least 30 minutes longer than the latter.

HOW DOES MY YEAR PARTNER (IF I HAVE ONE) LIKE TO WORK?

This is possibly the most important thing to consider, especially if you're like me (or work with someone like me) who, once the overview is nicely sorted, just gets on with the work, headphones on, the Elvis NBC TV special in my ears. I suggest that you discuss your preferred approaches from the start and ensure that your plan is something you can both stick to. For example, while I listen to music, I have no issue discussing ideas/problems as we work and trying to resolve them together. Between tracks.

DO I NEED TO BRING ANYTHING TO THE PPA SESSION?

This is especially pertinent towards the end of term/half-term when you may need to consider upcoming topics. Make sure you arrive with whatever you agreed to bring so that no precious time is wasted.

WHAT AM I HAPPY TO CONTINUE/ COMPLETE OUTSIDE OF PPA?

A reality for many colleagues is that – no matter how efficient they are – an entire morning or afternoon session of PPA will rarely be enough time to plan lessons for the entire week, differentiate plans for children who need extra support or further stretch and challenge, create or locate resources to support the plans, print off resources and plan for next week's PPA. So, know what you *must* get done before the end of the PPA session and what you can take home. It will vary for different colleagues, so I can't advise here – just make sure the question is asked.

WHAT DO I NEED TO PLAN IN MOST DETAIL?

Recognising your own needs is as important as recognising those of the children, and accepting that there are some subjects in which you will require more of a script compared to others is important. For me, as a trained PE teacher, I need less time to plan PE, but in history, in which I encourage more Socratic enquiry from the children, I need to spend a bit more time on planning. This is an invaluable reflection. Make sure you use it so you don't waste time.

WORKING SMARTER TIPS

LET CROSS-CURRICULAR LEARNING HELP YOUR PLANNING

Once you have examined your curriculum in detail, along with your accompanying school curriculum plan, with a careful eye on literacy skills development – that is reading *and* writing – working in a cross-curricular way becomes a much more straightforward process. This is made even easier if you put reading at the heart of *all* subjects, not treat it as a stand-alone lesson. This gives it real purpose and offers the children immediate access to a wide range of genres.

Making your learning cross-curricular will also allow you to plan appropriate writing opportunities for your history, geography, science and RE lessons (I would recommend enquiry-based, destination questions for this – see page 59). This not only provides a perfect opportunity to meet the need to write for a range of purposes and audiences but also incorporates elements of spelling, punctuation and grammar that you have worked on – creating perfect tie-ins.

This is particularly true at the top end of primary school, but can easily be applied throughout primary learning. This way of working can provide purpose, audience and specific learning opportunities – rather than esoteric stand-alone lessons – and it also saves time. If you plan for writing across the curriculum, you don't always have to have specific writing lessons for their own sake, making more time for writing, or, indeed, other important classroom activities.

Apart from narratives and stories, consider the various genres of writing you want to cover:

- Letters.
- Diaries.
- Non-chronological reports.
- Recounts.
- Poems.
- Dialogue/speeches.
- Explanations.

- Instructions.

- Persuasion.

Consider how you could deliver these through your foundation subjects.

Similarly, with numeracy you will find many opportunities to work in a cross-curricular manner if you look. Do you really need to dedicate a whole week, or even a few days, to charts when you cover this in science? Does ordering numbers need to be done in isolation when history presents perfect opportunities to do this through chronology? What about measuring, not only in science and food and nutrition, but also in athletics in PE? The later also lends itself nicely to converting between metres and centimetres.

Of course, I am not saying *never* teach stand-alone reading, writing, grammar or maths lessons. Far from it. These skills have to be taught and will need their own time and space. What I am suggesting, however, is how to make the most of the learning time in your class, and make your planning more effective, by *combining* learning opportunities, making them more relevant and memorable.

To illustrate this point, let me give you an example from my own class of 7- and 8-year-olds. Their writing task was to answer the question, 'Which group of invaders or settlers had the biggest impact on Britain?' This clearly came from our history curriculum, but through this enquiry question we were able to cover the following:

- Paragraphs – each invader/settler was given their own paragraph, detailing their achievements, their impact on Britain and how that impact is still seen today. In this way, paragraphs and the *purpose* behind them was easy for me to teach and for the children to understand.

● Commas – in lists, for example, of Roman foods.

● Conjunctions – having to make a judgement required the use of 'because'. When we coupled this with contrasting views we also brought in 'but', 'although' and 'however'. We even had the odd 'so' and 'therefore' thrown in for good measure.

● Prepositions – mainly 'before' and 'after', allowing the children to have a tangible understanding and immediate application of the words as they referenced the chronology.

Furthermore, because we were writing from a historical perspective, we included evidence. So the children learned about using quotes – for example, when referencing Tacitus' colourful remarks about Queen Boudicca.[2] This writing, being non-fiction, also meant that the children included subheadings, images and bulleted or numerical lists to make their work genre specific. Plus, there was the added bonus of covering geographical information about the peoples and where they settled.

All of this required reading and the specific teaching of the history and geography, as well as the English, to understand what they were going to write about and how they were going to write. However, all of the teaching was driven by the final piece, allowing the children to be able to access the learning, answer the question and meet the success criteria, which *they* had laid out. It also made (some of) them realise that *all* writing was important, that

2   See https://www.history.org.uk/primary/categories/315/module/2854/was-boudicca-britains-first-hero/2858/how-important-was-boudicca-in-the-romano-british-p.

writing is not just about stories and that effective written communication requires correct spelling, punctuation and grammar, and good handwriting, regardless of the subject.

WORKING SMARTER TIPS

PLAN FOR EVERY CHILD

Again, this may seem obvious but, let's be honest, does it really happen? *Really?*

Consider my previous points about joint/shared planning and/or whole-school/downloaded plans and you'll recall that, no matter how good these are, they will not fully address the needs of your class. Furthermore, it would be impossible for them to recognise every individual in your class, yet is this not the ultimate aim of our most effective planning?

If you suggest that planning for true diversity is neither feasible nor possible, I'd like to suggest the following considerations:

- What if *your* child was in your class? Would you be happy that he or she wasn't being identified as an individual, but as part of some homogenous mass – possibly somewhere towards the middle of the class' bell curve?

- If, as I have suggested, you know the journey for the subject/topic and you also know the needs and requirements of the children in your class, then why not marry the two to ensure that your planning is detailed and focused? In this way, the best planning will allow you to consider the subject, the topic, the learning focus and the children simultaneously. This will also allow you to ensure that every child meets challenges, has successes and encounters failure, while making progress in their learning.

I know that this scares many people. I also know that many people think it is impossible to meet the needs of all 30 or so children. I assure you, however, that this will fundamentally be down to the design and preparation of the resources to offer scaffolding, support and challenge (which we'll return to in a moment).

As you can see, I feel that these elements – knowing your curriculum well, planning for cross-curricular delivery and planning for *every* child, combined with joint PPA where possible – are the fundamentals for successful planning.

However, you also need to ask yourself ...

DO WE HAVE A CLEAR CURRICULUM MAP?

This would usually be constructed for every subject and would show what is being taught – by topic or theme – across the academic year. The curriculum coordinator and/or subject leaders will have had major input into this as it will provide clear reference points about where the learners have come from and where they are going to, as well as where they currently are on their learning journey.

This will then allow for your individual input into the delivery of the content, which shouldn't be too detailed or onerous, but should provide a clear route through the topic and give you an idea of what's to come. If you're in a year group team, it is best to construct this together. This will save time when it comes to weekly PPA and the planning of individual lessons.

Personally, I prefer to have this set out for the entire academic year before the end of the previous academic year. Fortunately, my Year 6 colleague prefers to work in this way too, so there is no need to find a compromise. In this way, we have a clear vision for the coming year. Although, termly overviews can also work just fine, if that's your preference. Whichever you decide upon, this can be easily communicated to parents. The level of detail is down to you, but you can always include suggestions of landmarks/museums/books/TV shows/films/websites which will help parents to support their children with the learning that they will encounter.

DO WE HAVE A WEEKLY OVERVIEW?

Use your curriculum map to create weekly overviews for all subjects. This is especially important for literacy, so that it can be built in across the curriculum. Working like this is just the ticket when it comes to joint PPA. Discuss where you all are in relation to the termly overview and identify any issues you had. Were they the same? How did you each resolve them? Are they completely resolved? Then you can check progress and look at the week ahead, before planning for your classes, addressing anything from the current week that needs to be reactivated, reviewed or developed.

DO I USE A CLASS TIMELINE FOR HISTORY, TO WHICH NEW LEARNING IS ADDED TO MAKE ITS PLACE OVERT FOR THE CHILDREN?

If you want to reinforce the chronology of the learning in history, this is great to consider when introducing a new piece of learning. Not only does it enable you to look at where it needs to be added in the timeline, but it also serves to reactivate prior learning. This prior learning not only relates to what you have taught so far this year but what the children will have covered in previous years too. For example, where would the Ancient Greeks be on your timeline, compared to the Egyptians? I ensure that we use a class timeline – ours is actually consistent across the school – and then we can place each new period of history onto it, creating chronological understanding and context – for example, recognising that Tudors and Aztecs were contemporaries, rather than the children thinking the Aztecs were an ancient civilization.

WHO AM I PLANNING FOR?

Remember that plans are for you (and your LSA – more on that in Chapter 6, but suffice to say they should see *and* understand your plans) so don't write them to please anyone else, especially an external body.

DO I PLAN MY QUESTIONS?

Clearly, not every question you ask in a lesson can be planned, but knowing the main focus and, more importantly, who you're going to ask is an invaluable tool in your kit. If you're providing a stimulus, it will be for a purpose, so think about what you're trying to elicit, evoke or provoke and consider the questions and the language you will use. (As an aside, it is this level of planning that has led colleagues to claim that I 'wing it' when teaching. Like the best Morecambe and Wise routine or Alan Partridge bit, even the off-the-cuff asides are all carefully planned.)

Through this careful planning, you can ensure that the lesson flows well and you manage to include *everyone* at an appropriate level. This includes considering your follow-up questions and those designed to interrogate expected answers to delve even deeper.

HOW OFTEN DO I GO WITH THE FLOW?

To paraphrase a famous quote, planning is important, but plans can be a waste of time. Sometimes you need to be prepared to ditch the plan and wing it. This is when some of your best teaching will happen, I promise.

Winging it successfully happens when you plan well enough to be able to allow the class to take things in a different direction. Thanks to having considered these questions, and having detailed plans and knowledge of the subject safely in my back pocket, I can be confident that I can go with the flow, see where it leads and then get everyone back on track for a story before you can say 'Biff, Chip and Kipper'.

RESOURCES

WORKING SMARTER TIPS

USE ONLINE RESOURCES SPARINGLY

I'm not saying *never* use them, but if you want all the benefits of making your lessons as bespoke as possible, then an online 'click and print' site is only storing up trouble for you further down the line. Acknowledging how hard-pressed primary colleagues are, who am I to say never, ever use pre-made resources? Just tread carefully. Is the resource you've found online an essential part of the learning or just a filler? (Mindful colouring I'm looking at you.)

Notwithstanding this concern, I would ask you: how many resources do you or, more importantly, the children *need*?

To me, many colleagues spend an inordinate amount of time preparing (yes, I know that's partly what PPA is for), printing, guillotining, laminating and displaying resources. From here we are only a hop, skip and a jump away from all-out in early for photocopying (IEFP) syndrome! To help combat this pernicious disease, here are some questions to consider before we swipe our pass on the printer key-pad and hit the '3' and the '0' keys, so that every child gets one.

DO I ACTUALLY NEED A RESOURCE?

Make sure you ask yourself this before you print or copy, or – better still – before you search for or create a resource. If a resource is not really necessary or, worse, not the *best* way to support learning, then put the master copy down and step away from the photocopier.

WHAT DO I ALREADY HAVE THAT I COULD USE?

Most classrooms will already have a plethora of resources that could be put to cross-curricular use. Maths resources are a particular favourite of mine to rehome. A bead string is a great resource for chronology in history, for example, charting key dates in Britain up to, or even after, 1066. This can aid counting in tens, as each bead becomes 10 years and (with 100) you can cover 1,000 years of history quite easily, identifying key events and people across history. Doing this allows you to show how far apart events are (e.g. the Battle of Hastings and the start of the Tudors' reign – separated by 419 years – are separated by 42 beads) and allows for dialogue supported by a tangible resource, which we can keep coming back to. As the children count the beads, they can create a space on the string, where they place a sticky note to show the exact date of the start and end of a historic period (e.g. 1485 for the Battle of Bosworth to 1603 for the death of Elizabeth I for the Tudors). Just think about how many ways you could repurpose Dienes (or base ten) blocks, Cuisenaire rods, counting sticks, tens frames, dice, playing cards and the likes for other parts of the curriculum. (There's an INSET day activity if ever there was one!)

WHAT CAN THE CHILDREN CREATE?

Too many teachers work far harder than the children they teach. But then you know that; that's why you're reading this book. There are more of them than you and each of them can contribute to the class' resources. One perfect example would be the creation of flashcards, especially for times tables. In this way you have:

- A lesson in and of itself.

- A way to develop creativity.

- A way to support the class' memorisation of the tables.

- And a way to ensure that the children take care of the resources and use them frequently.

Another great example, which I use across subjects, would be the class creation of Top Trumps cards. This is made easier if you use Google Docs or an equivalent app and is a perfect piece of early morning work for 'The settle'. You just have to create a template and sit back.

ARE YOU REINVENTING THE WHEEL?

Look at your school's shared computer drive (I know, it could take months!). The fact that many schools have such drives allows you to find resources that others have lovingly and painstakingly created, which can at least act as a starting point for your class.

Not everyone will save work in a logical format. Save yourself even more time – especially if the drive is a bit of a mess – by talking to whoever has taught the topic before (a curriculum map should help here). Their resources may not have been for the same year group, but will give you a starting point. When it comes to adding your material to the drive, make sure you label your resources clearly and accurately. Use your own system, but including the topic and title would seem best if you're going to support those who will teach the topic after you.

WHAT'S MY BUDGET?[3]

If you're not a subject leader/budget holder, it is vital that you know what you can spend. As I have said, knowing what is actually in your curriculum is key here, and watch out for the snake oil salespeople. Know what you're supposed to be teaching and, from there, how any purchase will support the learning, especially if you are given a hefty budget to play with. (Ah, the good old days.)

It is always good form to bear in mind that although it is not your money, you should treat it like it is. The school have trusted you with this precious, limited and diminishing resource, so spend it wisely. Avoid buying the shiny and sparkly just for the sake of it, especially – with an eye for modelling good environmental practice – if it's a single-use item.

WHAT'S IN MY LOCAL AREA?

Rather than purchasing resources, could you use the locality, environment and local community? Rather than purchase a set of cards about habitats, for example, take the children into local habitats, whether that's a park, wood or garden. Could the school cultivate its own outdoor

---

3 A note on budgets. In my experience, too many people wait until towards the end of the financial year before spending their allowance - especially as many schools will 'freeze' budgets in advance of the new financial year. This means that the children are losing out on their entitlement. If you're a budget holder, I'd expect at least half of the budget to be spent by the start of September (having received it at Easter) and then for it to be virtually all gone by Christmas. A way to ensure a focus on spending would be to monitor it year on year. Don't just leave it to the business/finance manager. Know what's being delivered across the school, know what stock resources the school already has, and plan ahead.

area? Many EYFS facilities have them, so why not throughout the school? With many schools getting involved in outdoor learning, especially post pandemic, look to cultivate your own sensory garden/nature reserve/ pond, etc. If this concept is new to you, check out the excellent work of Independent Thinking Associate Juliet Robertson, starting with *Dirty Teaching*.[4]

HOW CAN THE INTERNET HELP ME?

No, not with finding resources! How can you bring learning to life without printing anything off? Many of us had to go online to see the world thanks to the pandemic restricting trips/visits/visitors, so what impact could websites like Google Earth or Google Arts & Culture have in your classroom? Both not only transport your children to new places, but also allow the children to explore *for themselves*.

MARKING AND FEEDBACK

I know that for many colleagues this is a thorny issue. I have heard of schools that have a triple marking policy, in which the teacher marks the work, the pupil responds and then the teacher responds to the response. I think you know me well enough by now to predict my response to that approach. Ultimately, you and your SLT need to decide whether you follow the myths about marking (the inspectors need it/parents expect it/we must do more of it to get grades up) or the research, which tends to go the way of 'less is more' when it comes to feedback to learners.

---

4 J. Robertson, *Dirty Teaching: A Beginner's Guide to Learning Outdoors* (Carmarthen: Independent Thinking Press, 2014).

WORKING SMARTER TIPS

READ THE RESEARCH

If you have always thought that marking books during evenings and weekends is all part of what you signed up for as a committed teacher then, take a seat, as you might find what I am about to say alarming.

You've been misled.

Perhaps the research is best summed up by the Education Endowment Foundation (EEF), which advocates a 'no written marking' policy.[5] Marking that traditionally happens *after* the lesson is the very poor relation of the feedback that takes place immediately during the lesson. So, grab your diary and address book and plan your new-found social life. Stop wasting your life marking books when you can focus instead on delivering high-quality, targeted feedback during working hours, five days a week.

---

5 V. Elliot et al., *A Marked Improvement? A Review of the Evidence on Written Marking* (London: Education Endowment Foundation, 2016). Available at: https://educationendowmentfoundation.org.uk/education-evidence/evidence-reviews/written-marking; J. Collin and A. Quigley, *Teacher Feedback to Improve Pupil Learning: Guidance Report* (London: Education Endowment Foundation, 2021). Available at: https://educationendowmentfoundation.org.uk/education-evidence/guidance-reports/feedback#nav-download-the-guidance-report-and-poster.

WHO IS THE MARKING FOR?

As with lesson planning, too often our answer to this question indicates that we are looking in the wrong place. Marking is 100% for the child involved. Simple as. Therefore, when marking – better still, let's call it what it should be: feedback – consider the following:

- What are your non-negotiables? Never correct errors that the class is well aware they should be looking out for and avoiding (see the advice that follows for more on this controversial approach).

- What was the purpose and focus of the learning? Target your feedback *specifically* here.

- Are there common errors that most/all of the class are making? This is great feedback for you as the one who either created misconceptions or let them linger. Use this insight to target tomorrow's teaching, even if it involves setting up a smaller group to address how and where these misunderstandings grew.

CHANGE THE LEARNER, NOT THE WORK

My Independent Thinking colleague and restorative practice guru Mark Finnis talks about the 'power of with' and what happens when you do things 'with' children and not 'to' them or 'for' them. My response to them neglecting the non-negotiables comes very much under the 'with' banner. You have made your expectations clear, so stick to them. If a child presents work that contravenes one or more non-negotiable –

and a quick scan will enable you to spot any infractions – simply hand the book back and ask them to look again. The lessons they are learning about taking responsibility for their work go well beyond whatever grammar or style point you might be making. You can encourage them to ask peers for support if they can't see their mistake – another 'with' process in which everyone wins.

Furthermore, rather than have the children edit their own work, which then creates another 30 or so pieces of marking/feedback for you, why not create an example piece of work with errors that you want the children to edit? That way you can:

● Target the work to the specific learning purpose.

● Include common errors that you saw when reviewing the books.

● Check the work easily as you create the work with errors and the children all review the piece simultaneously. They then check their own/a peer's work against the model you have created, with all your deliberate errors easily highlighted. Did the children spot them? What was missed? Do they agree? From this, you are clearly informed about the children's ability to retain learning and their ability to spot errors, without you having to mark 30 pieces of individual work.

In my view, this will be one of the best resources you can create – especially if you include some shades of grey to provoke discussion.

MAKE THE MOST OF WHAT YOU ALREADY DO

'It ain't what you do,' yadda, yadda, yadda. Look at what you are doing anyway and have a think about how you can change the way in which you are doing it to improve the impact. For example:

- Like a gardener circling the borders with a hoe, circulate the room and catch any errors as they emerge. Addressing these weeds before they take root makes your intervention far more relevant and helpful for the children concerned. You can also make a call as to whether you need to set up a brief whole-class or small group reteach if the problem is a common one.

- Remember marking/feedback isn't only about catching errors. Celebrate as you circulate. Using your visualiser (if you have one) to share examples of good work is powerful. In doing so, you have created another model to support the whole class.

- Deploy your LSA effectively as they should be providing feedback too. Of course, your communication and their confidence have a part to play here, so work on both.

- Use word mats or word banks to minimise the time you spend on spelling corrections. Simply refer the children to the resource (which they could also create, by the way).

- Target spellings – a sticky-note-based system is ideal for this, so the children can keep a list of their common errors in their book for reference. I get the children to tick off words when they subsequently use them in other pieces of work. Using sticky notes is great because they can be transferred between books.

● Allow time. If you want feedback to be effective, give it the time it deserves. Especially early in the academic year, time spent on feedback is an investment and will pay off later as it becomes part of your everyday habits and practice.

'Love your ideas, Mark, but have you met my SLT?'

For those of you who are working in a regime in which marking books, wasting time and waving your family goodbye after Sunday lunch is what is expected, then here are some pointers that might help:

● Move to another school! No, really, that is my number one tip. Why would you want to work in a school where they are adding this burden to your workload, especially if it involves triple marking? Looking after your own health and well-being has to be your number one priority, otherwise you can't be effective. If the SLT ask why you want to leave, tell them – point them to the research. Remember, you won't be alone in wanting something drastic to change. The young teacher I met at a course recently who had to mark every single book every day would certainly be in your corner.

● Read and research, then present the information to them. Could you run an in-house research project to show the SLT and the wider school community the benefits of a different approach? (Again, the EEF research is a powerful ally here, not to mention reaching out to schools that have already successfully travelled this path.)

- Check the actual wording of your school's marking policy and, like a government minister getting themselves off the hook about giving out that dodgy contract, find a way around it. For example, one school I worked in claimed to be strict on marking, insisting that 'every' piece of work had to receive feedback. I trained the children well in peer assessment (the policy didn't actually say that the feedback had to be from an adult) as well as upskilling my LSA (it didn't say the teacher had to do it either). I also simplified my marking and feedback using highlighter pens. I opted for a simple two-colour system: green = good; pink = think. This had the added benefit of putting the onus on the child to take their work back and apply themselves a bit more.

If you are happy where you are, don't want to cause a fuss and would only like to see your family a little more often but not all the time, may I suggest two final points:

- Use your time wisely and don't waste it. If you're marking, focus on the school policy, meet that expectation and get it done quickly. Ditto the lesson's success criteria. Without this cut-off, it can all become too much.

- Remember, there's always more that can be done so have a clear limit for yourself. Set a time and place to mark, have a system for marking and stick to it. I may prefer reviewing books at school to avoid taking them home, but others would rather leave earlier and mark later from the comfort of their own gin and tonic.

THAT 'F' WORD AGAIN

The good Dr. Seuss[6] summed it up perfectly when he wrote:

If you never did, you should.

These things are fun, and fun is good.[7]

WORKING SMARTER TIPS

MAKE LEARNING FUN!

That's it, in essence. Not sure how else to put it.

Empirical evidence (think about training courses you have been on or that INSET day that seemed to last a week) and the research (check out, for example, *The Little Book of Big Stuff About the Brain* by Dr Andrew Curran[8]) tell us what some seem to want to deny – if we are engaged and happy then the stuff we are learning sticks.

My view is that it is down to the adults in the room – and not just the teacher – to build as much fun as is possible into the learning to improve the quality and stickiness of that learning as well as improve motivation, enhance social interactions, strengthen

---

6   Not a real doctor.

7   Dr. Seuss, *One Fish, Two Fish, Red Fish, Blue Fish* (New York: Random House, 1960), p. 51.

8   A real doctor and a paediatric neurologist at that. A. Curran, *The Little Book of Big Stuff About the Brain: The True Story of Your Amazing Brain* (Carmarthen: Crown House Publishing, 2008).

relationships and remind us of our common, linked humanity.

Throughout the book I've guided you in ways of having fun in class, using games and Thunks are just two I've (hopefully) sneaked past you, so, when considering how you approach having fun, ask yourself ...

AM I HAVING FUN?

No one is asking you to play the clown or do anything you feel uncomfortable with (but a smile before Christmas wouldn't kill you). Childhood can be a magical time and you get to be part of hundreds of childhoods in a way a bank manager or car mechanic never will. And, remember, if you're enjoying yourself, tell your face, as the old trainer's entreaty goes.

DO I EVER GO WITH THE FLOW?

Remember my advice about planning and be prepared to allow moments of serendipity to flower. Your plan details where you intend to start and need to finish but there could well be unexpected gold in the wiggly bit in-between.

HOW OFTEN DO I LAUGH?

There is a lot of truth in the saying, 'Your day will go in the direction of the corners of your mouth.' Furthermore, while the research behind it is debated, there is a weight of belief behind the assertion that children laugh more than adults.[9] And look how young they look!

WHEN DID I LAST LAUGH IN CLASS?

Again, one for the 'with' not 'at' approach, unless you're laughing at yourself. Let the children make you laugh. Laugh at what they find funny, even if you aren't genuinely amused yourself. Be prepared to join in. Listen to and learn from the children. The best sound in my classroom is laughter, not silence.

DO I TAKE TIME TO SMELL THE METAPHORICAL ROSES?

If you are already picking up hints from this book to help you work smarter rather than harder, then you will soon start to have more time to stand still and take stock. Enjoy the moment. Be present. Stop and observe. In your mind's eye, float above the classroom and see yourself there with a group of happy, learning children and enjoy it. It's what you said you always wanted and here it is.[10]

HOW DO I PROVOKE THE CLASS' FUNNY BONE?

Where to start? Telling jokes, reading from a book of funny rhymes or poems, watching a funny YouTube or TikTok clip (either of your choice or theirs, just check their choice first), listening to music, creating little sketches and using drama techniques, magic tricks, puzzles, juggling, etc. All of these approaches and more can be used either to

---

9   R. A. Martin, Do Children Laugh Much More Often Than Adults Do? *Association for Applied and Therapeutic Humor* (n.d.). Available at: https://aath.memberclicks.net/do-children-laugh-much-more-often-than-adults-do.

10 Of course, if you pause and start to question what the hell you've done with your life, then maybe it's time for a rethink.

enhance the learning with a little creative thinking or as part of a learning break.

What about the games you already have at your disposal – such as the ones that only come out when the head's messenger puts their face around the door and hands you the note with the immortal words: 'Wet play'? What's more, getting children to make their own games has so many learning benefits. One class I taught created their own game called *Coniecto Qui* (no, you work it out – if my 9-year-olds can use Google Translate, so can you) based on their learning about the Romans.

CHAPTER CONTEMPLATIONS

This chapter has been all about what goes on in our classrooms and how to make our use of time as successful and effective as possible. I feel that there is lots of advice out there about how to teach, but I have aimed here to focus on what I see as the four key elements – planning, resources, marking and fun – that you can work smarter at to ensure you can teach successfully.

Driving this, as ever, are four important questions:

- What do I do?

- How do I do it?

- Why do I do it that way?

- How else *could* I do it?

To which I would add the following for you to consider:

- Do I make time to find out what the research says about effective practice?

- What do the inspectors *really* say about ...?

- What are the justifications behind whole-school practices, and can they be questioned (or subverted)?

- How well do I and my colleagues know what is really in the curriculum? (And what would happen if we, you know, miss out a few bits here and there ...?)

And, for me, the most important consideration of all:

- Do I start each day with an optimistic outlook and end it the same way, able to reflect positively on my successes and healthily on what didn't go so well? Or does each day make me wish I was doing something easier, like an Ironman race or negotiating a post-Brexit trade deal?

If you find that you are too often in the latter category (we are all in there some of the time, let's be honest) then I hope this book is helping you come to the realisation that there genuinely and always is another way.

CHAPTER 3

LEARNING OUTSIDE THE CLASSROOM

I have opened with two chapters all about the room where learning happens, but how can we be smarter in our work outside the classroom? And yes, that is your domain too, so stop thinking of things like playground duty as an opportunity to drink coffee in the rain and more as an opportunity to really raise the bar when it comes to smart working.

There are three main beyond-the-classroom areas I want to focus on in this chapter:

1   Playtime.

2   Lunchtime.

3   (Un)homework.

First off, having written previously about the burden of teacher workload, you could be forgiven for thinking that my advice would be to be like Elsa and let it go. While this approach, in the short term, would free up time and reduce workload, in the longer term such respite is temporary and is far outweighed by the benefits of exploiting these opportunities for some seriously smart working.

PLAYTIME

Never ever forget that playtime is something very special in a primary school. In big school they don't mention play and simply call it 'break', which is the sort of thing you get halfway through the ITV news or what boxers do when they're getting tired. Not to mention how 'lunchtime' becomes 'lunch break', something that is being squeezed into an ever-smaller amount of the school day to 'free up' more time for learning, supposedly. So, if for no other reason than because it is something special at primary school and has the word 'play' in it, let's celebrate it, cherish it, and ensure that we approach playtime in a meaningfully playful way.

I recognise that this time of the day brings with it huge potential for causing stress, both for your pupils and, consequently, for you, regardless of whether you are the one on duty. However, the mindset with which you approach these events will determine a great deal of what happens next. And although you can't control a full-scale outbreak of 'He said ... But she said ... Well, he said ...', you can at least control your mindset, not to mention some of the routines you can introduce.

WORKING SMARTER TIPS

GET THE CHILDREN OUT PROMPTLY

Again, at the risk of provoking a 'Well, duh!' response, please make sure you know (and keep track of) when playtime and lunchtime actually start, especially if you share the play space with other classes. Remember, not only do you need a respite from the work, so do the children. Ensure your class aren't delayed heading out, especially if they have to be back in promptly, so they can have their full playtime and let off the steam they need to. This serves to continue the general sense of purpose you will have instilled in your class; playtime is just another aspect of the day with the same clear expectations and non-negotiables. Being on time with playtime and lunchtime will also help you to identify the 'clock watchers',[1] who you can use to your advantage by putting them in charge of monitoring your punctuality.

CARRY WORK OVER TO AFTER PLAYTIME

As with assemblies, having work to go back to after playtime and lunchtime, even if you're going to be moving on to something new in ten minutes or so, helps in a number of ways:

● It helps with settling the children, preventing time wasting.

● It reactivates their brain with familiar work.

● It allows you to prepare for the next lesson (essential if you have been on duty).

---

1   Do keep an eye out for these children as their behaviour could be hiding a safeguarding concern. I once learned about a domestic abuse situation as a result of a child's anxiety about everything being on time. It turned out that his father could get physically abusive if dinner was not on the table at the right time.

- It gives you time if you do need to 'have a word' with anyone.

This has also been great during the seemingly non-stop handwashing time introduced by the pandemic. The children can come in and get on with something meaningful (and not 'just read') while their peers finish their ablutions.

WALK WITH A PURPOSE

Expecting my class to get from the classroom to the playground and back again swiftly and promptly, as if I mean business (because I do), does not make me an advocate for silent corridors. What it does make me is someone who expects his class to know that playtime or lunchtime is over and that we are all getting back to work now. I think the nature of the transition sets the tone for the learning that will follow, especially if you follow the previous tip about carrying work over. You simply remind the children about what they're returning to, while taking the opportunity to highlight to those children who need it that you'll be checking in with them when you're all back in the room for extra support, extension tasks or simply a progress update.

PLAY WITH THE CHILDREN

If you are expected to undertake playground duty, then get involved with the children. Don't just stand around chatting to colleagues and ignoring the children. I do appreciate that this can be tough in some schools, as it's almost an unwritten rule that the adults will huddle together while playtime goes on around them, and breaking this convention will be hard. But I would seriously advocate that playing with the children should be the main purpose of being on duty at playtime.

Teachers and parents frequently moan that many children spend too long indoors on their devices, rather than outside getting fresh air and exercise, so let's model to them how important outdoor play is. Joining in with games means a lot to the children, especially if they are teaching you the game they are playing. Does your playground have a painted hopscotch grid? If not, take some chalk outside and make one. Games don't take a lot of effort. 'Splat', for example, is great to play and you can work your way around different groups of children, maximising your input to children beyond your own class (although don't ignore your learners as they might take it personally). For the uninitiated, to play the game:

1 The players stand in a circle with one person in the middle.

2 The person in the middle will spin round and, at random, point to one player and shout 'splat'.

3 This player ducks down and the two people either side of them point at each other and shout 'splat'.

4 The second person to shout 'splat' sits down. (Note: if someone says 'splat' but they are not either side of the splatted player, they're out and have to sit down too.)

5 The game continues until there are only two players remaining. They should stand

back-to-back, duel style, and when signalled walk away from each other.

6   When the person leading (who was in the middle) shouts 'splat', the last two players have to turn and shout 'splat' at each other. The first to shout is the winner – if they turn pre-emptively, they lose.

Even if you are not expected to undertake duty, make sure you get out on the playground and get involved every so often. You will add another pair of eyes to the duty team, and what's more, you will be role-modelling what you believe in. And, no, I'm not just advocating doing this in the summer when you want to show off your cool shades and top up your tan.

Given that the premise of this book is all about making your life easier, I appreciate that, on the face of it, the advice to make time to play may go against the grain. However, the truth is quite different. This time together allows you to get to know your children, to see them in a different context and to begin to break down any barriers. It will give you quiet moments, allowing you to chat to them and, in this different context, you will often find them more willing to share their troubles and concerns with you. It also creates a non-threatening environment in which you can chat about learning, how they're doing and what they're thinking. Chatting while turning a skipping rope is simple and, with the distraction of the game, a lot can be revealed if you're prepared to listen.

So, when considering how you approach playtime, ask yourself ...

DO I REALLY PAY ATTENTION TO MY CLASS AS THEY GO OUT?

What follows is not an exhaustive list but a handy guide to pre-empting potential issues that you would otherwise have to mop up afterwards. So, in your class, do you know:

- Who dawdles to get out?

- Who hangs around the classroom offering to help?

- Who seems upset?

- Who is particularly loud?

- Who is particularly quiet?

- Who has fallen out with whom already today?

- Who has been having whispered conversations during the morning?

- Who is asking people to play with them before even getting outside?

- Who is clutching onto their friends, and do you know why? It could be for security but could also be a way of ensuring that someone else is left out.

- Who doesn't have a snack?

- Who is asking to swap or share food?

- Who is wanting to take something like a toy or a notebook outside?

DO I REALLY PAY ATTENTION TO MY CLASS AS THEY COME IN?

This is similar to the previous list but, again, do you know the answers and, more importantly, the reasons behind the behaviours?

- Who dawdles to get in?

- Who seems upset?

- Who is particularly loud?

- Who is particularly quiet?

- Who has fallen out during playtime and why?

- Who is asking people to play with them at lunchtime?

- Who is hungry?

- Who wants to go to the toilet?

- Who has left something outside?

With both lists, I would advocate being mindful of the frequency of the behaviour. A child coming in from playtime and needing the toilet is not an issue in and of itself (some may disagree), but the same child doing it every day? Note, too, that many of these questions are easier to answer if you have been out with them at playtime.

DO I WATCH MY CLASS FOR AT LEAST SOME OF PLAYTIME?

Even if you are not going out to play with them, and no matter how desperate your need for a caffeine fix, take a few minutes to go outside and keep a weather eye on your class. Watch their interactions and be ready to go and speak to anyone who is giving you cause for concern. Yes, I admit, you may miss more of your break than you intended, but ultimately the children will know that you care, plus you will usually save yourself the time and trouble it takes trying to unpick a 'he said, she said' argument after break.

Finishing your break a few minutes ahead of time and getting out to the playground is another timesaver in the long run. When observing your class, ask yourself:

- Who is engaging with whom?
- Who are the loners?
- Who isn't playing with anyone from their own class?
- Who is playing with younger children?
- Who is lost in a world of creativity?
- Who is running around 'like a loon' (there's always one)?
- Who is being bossy?
- Who is being subservient?
- Who is so busy arguing about the rules of a game they are missing out on playing it?
- Who *has* to win?
- Who are the peacemakers?
- Who responds to the bell or whistle most promptly?

The responses to these questions will not only tell you a lot about your class, they will provide valuable information when a parent talks to you about their child. Furthermore, it provides you with a fuller picture of your class and also allows you to plan lessons or activities to address/challenge/support any behaviours you have seen. For example, constructing a game based on chance for those who *have to* win is ideal, as is creating group activities with allocated roles – why not make the bossiest child the scribe? These interventions will help the children develop socially too.

LUNCHTIME

While much of this advice for breaktime is clearly applicable at lunchtime too, I think it is also worth adding some lunchtime-specific pointers.

WORKING SMARTER TIPS

EAT WITH THE CHILDREN

I know, I know. But in the same way that being on the playground gives you the chance to associate with the children beyond the classroom, with all the benefits that brings, eating with the children has numerous benefits too (not to mention the Brownie points you'll get from the mealtime supervisors, who will appreciate another adult in the dining room):

- You can be the one adult they actually eat with. We know many children are missing out on this important element of life – children and adults 'breaking bread' and engaging in conversation, not screen time.

- By doing this you can also help them with important elements of social skills – such as table manners, using cutlery, not talking with their mouths full, sitting still, not bolting their food to get outside or dawdling over it to avoid going outside.

● You can just chat, getting to know them and their interests better.

● You can monitor what the children are eating, which will help you consider your afternoon lessons. If they are not eating much, are they likely to be able to run around? What if they are eating too much sugar? How will you burn this off before expecting docile compliance and sitting down for the afternoon?

● Linked to that, and given the proven links between nutrition, behaviour and learning,[2] you can model good eating habits. (My class are still astounded that I have five pieces of fruit every day at school, especially when I eat the skin of my kiwi fruit.)

● Your class will feel special, helping to cement a bond that will pay dividends back in the classroom.

By the way, you may be surprised to observe how such actions can provoke noises of disgruntlement from some of your colleagues. Undaunted, I simply explain why I do it and that I'm not expecting anyone else to. I believe in what I am doing and so feel OK with any waves I cause.[3] And remember, I'm not suggesting

---

2 See https://www.bda.uk.com/resource/diet-behaviour-and-learning-children.html.

3 Of course, your reward will come during that one enforced communal meal of the year – the Christmas lunch – during which your class will behave impeccably while your recalcitrant colleagues sit covered in turkey spittle.

being in the dining room for the entire lunch break, nor eating with the children every day.

VARY WHO YOU SIT WITH

If you do venture into the dining hall, take care to sit with different children each time and, yes, that includes the child who never shuts up, the one who eats loudly and the one with the snotty dribbles. This way you get the whole class onside, whereas if the pupils perceive that you have favourites it will have the opposite effect.

I have also found that it works well if I ask a different child to save me a seat each time, so I am guaranteed to sit with different children, rather than me sitting down and the class flocking to me – good for the ego, but liable to leave out those children who are slower to get to the hall.

HELP OUT

Another bonus of joining in at lunchtime is that lending a hand to the mealtime supervisors shows them that clearing and cleaning up is not beneath you. It also allows you to get to know them better, which can often pay off in the long run regarding how they deal with your pupils – including if they need to report any behaviour or concerns to you. It is also a great role-modelling opportunity, useful back in the classroom when dealing with the 'But it isn't mine' response to clearing up.

BE IN YOUR ROOM SOMETIMES

Some members of your class won't want to go out to play and there can be many reasons why. At least once a week allow them in your room with you. Just be aware of the following:

● Ensure that the children don't interpret the classroom as an open house which they can go into when you're not there.

● If you need or want to work, do so. The children are being granted space, not extra input from you, so make sure they understand the expectations.

● While understanding this, be prepared to keep your eyes and ears open. Notice who plays with whom, what they play, who reads, who really just wants to be with you, etc. – it's all instructive feedback for working effectively with your class.

● Make sure that the children don't think they need to do more work if they are in the classroom. This is playtime. You may have to stop what you are doing to initiate a game but, again, this will pay dividends for all concerned.

● Remember, at times it can be useful to give children time and space for work, especially if they do not have these luxuries at home.

Other lunchtime questions to consider to help you get to know your class better include:

- Who always appears to be ravenous before lunch?

- Who always seems lethargic in the afternoon?

- Does anyone seem to be inordinately slow at washing their hands before lunch?

- Does anyone eat furtively?[4]

- Who spends the entire lunchtime in the dining hall rather than going outside?

- Who, Oliver-like, always wants more?

- Who never clears their plate?

- Who can't use a knife and fork correctly, opting for a one-handed jab with a fork?

- Who can't sit still?

- Who eats their food quickly?[5]

- Does anyone not eat in the 'correct order' (i.e. who goes straight for the pudding option before the main)?

All of these observations will give you a real insight into your class and may serve to reveal some underlying issues you might otherwise miss.

---

4   This tends to be more of a packed lunch issue, in my experience, where the child partially opens their lunch box and sneaks food out. I have known this to be a sign of food/body issues and/or embarrassment about the contents.

5   I have already mentioned the children who 'bolt and go'. This is often done to get more time playing, but that isn't always the case. I have found that some children eat rapidly because there's a scarcity of food at home so they have learned that they have to be quick. In others, I have discovered that this habit revealed a body-image issue, even in quite young children.

UNHOMEWORK

Homework in primary schools is, as I say in my book *Unhomework*,[6] a Goldilocks issue for parents. I get around this with unhomework, which is my philosophy for addressing the burdens on children, parents and teachers around formal homework setting that too many of us are all too aware of. Unhomework is designed to achieve better results by not setting formal homework, but by tackling the expectation for home learning in a different, unhomework, way. Hereby the onus and responsibility for learning outside of the classroom is on the learner, not me, or the parents. Parents tend to fall into three main groups, each with their own individual and nuanced reasons for their stance:

1   There's not enough.

   ▲ 'We're chasing an eleven-plus result and grammar school.'

   ▲ 'I want to replicate my childhood experiences – it never did me any harm!'

   ▲ 'I don't want to have to bother with them when they get in from school. They need to be kept busy.'

   ▲ 'They'll get homework at secondary school, so they need to know what to expect.'[7]

2   There's too much.

   ▲ 'They do enough learning at school; they need to come home and be a child.'

   ▲ 'I don't want to replicate my childhood experiences – I always hated homework!'

---

6   M. Creasy, *Unhomework: How to Get the Most out of Homework without Really Setting It* (Carmarthen: Independent Thinking Press, 2014).

7   I heard this from a Year 2 parent once!

▲ 'They've got other things, like clubs, to do after school.'

▲ 'They'll get enough homework at secondary school; they don't need it now.'

▲ 'Why can't you just teach everything they need to know at school? That's your job, not mine.'

3 It's just about right.

In my experience, this third Goldilocks group can be broken down into three subsets:

1 Those who are happy with their child's progress and see the amount of homework they get as contributing to this.

2 Those who haven't got a clue what goes on.

3 Those who don't care.

Keep this in mind and keep at least half an eye on your school's homework policy, then think about how to be smart with your approaches to working outside of class.

For me, home learning should involve:

1 Times tables practice – *every night*.

2 Reading – *every night*, *to* the child, as well as *with* them.

That's it.

However, to cover your back, I would also recommend a third compulsory element:

3 Creative tasks. This is something the children can pick from a menu of options (see Appendix 1), that takes between two and three weeks to complete and culminates in a presentation to the class. During this time one of your roles is to monitor progress and the

nature of the work being created. (This will save you having to sit through countless pointless PowerPoint presentations or show-and-tells based on something they found in the road on the way to school.)

With this third element, I am using the word 'compulsory' carefully. Save your battles for points 1 and 2. The important part of point 3 is that the children enjoy it, and that it does not cause stress and unpleasantness at home. To help, you could provide time and resources for the children in school, but the holy grail of all home learning is the work the children do without you setting anything: work they do because you have inspired them to. This is the essence of unhomework.

It is also probably worth reflecting on some other points to consider when it comes to being smart about homework.

WORKING SMARTER TIPS

KNOW THE SCHOOL'S EXPECTATIONS

As with the marking policy I mentioned in Chapter 2, there's often a disconnect between the stated policy and the 'It's what we do here' culture. You're best placed to decide what to do, and you might even get away with just setting times tables practice and reading if you *know* the policy.

MODEL THE WORK

We do this all the time in English and maths when we show the children how things should be done, so the same should apply to home learning. This is especially the case when it will help teach them (and their parents) what you mean by instructions such as:

- Create a collage about ...

- Make a poster for ...

- Design a website on ...

- Make a model of ...

- Research and create a presentation about ...

You may feel you've covered this in class, but the parents weren't there and may interpret the task in their own sweet way. To help, I recommend that you create and share examples in class, then:

- Have them on display so that parents can come in and see them for reference.

- Include them on your class page on the school website. Over time, you can replace your examples with ones done by the children themselves.

- If your school uses Twitter (and I would thoroughly recommend having a closed group for each class), tweet them out.

- Email the pictures to parents or share them via other suitable applications.

USE TECHNOLOGY TO HELP YOU

Where possible – and with careful planning so no one perceives it as either you or the children 'copping out' – let tech take the strain. What follows is a list of some of the sites that I use, but do feel free to 'ask Twitter' for any more. These are my preferred options because the teacher's input and effort is minimal and they track and record the children's progress, allowing you to make adjustments as necessary.

- The Khan Academy (free).[8] Create your class, set work and then sit back as the system tracks it for you. There are even online tutorials, so there's no excuse of 'I didn't do it because I didn't understand/couldn't remember'.

- Google Forms (free).[9] If your school uses Google for email, you can create a multiple-choice quiz which the system will mark and score for you once you tell it the right answers. This is great for spelling and maths tests as well as for closed question memory-based reviews across all subjects.

- Times Tables Rock Stars (subscription – but won't break the school bank).[10] This is an interactive game where the teacher can set the tables for individual children, if they want, and the children practise them. Also, there are different functions to develop speed and fluency – for example, 'Soundcheck' has a six-second function built in, so answers have to be more rapid. Added to this is the ability to challenge other children in the

---

8 See https://www.khanacademy.org/.
9 See https://www.google.co.uk/forms/about/.
10 See https://ttrockstars.com/.

'Stadium' – you can decide whether they go up against the class, the whole school or any other Times Tables Rock Stars users anywhere in the world. All of this throws up so much useful data for the teacher, including a class/individual 'heat map', so the teacher can see the time being taken for individual calculations and understand where gaps/blocks are. This is, clearly, best done as a whole-school strategy – especially when paired with Numbots,[11] aimed at 5–8-year-olds for mental addition and subtraction – and follows the little and often model.

- Hit the Button (free online or download the app).[12] There are many ways to use this tool in whichever version (I'm a tightwad so the free website is good for me). It also includes some added bonuses, such as games involving number bonds and decimals. I've directed many parents to this site, especially as it's a timed game, and, with each game lasting only one minute, ten minutes of tables practice every night is easy to track for the parents.

- Timestables (free online).[13] Although there is no teacher tracking facility, this is ideal to supplement what's going on in class. The real benefit is that the children can:

  ▲ Select the table they want to practise – you will need to ensure that they understand they are to practise the tables they need to improve at, not simply rack up high scores on the 2, 5 and 10 times tables.

---

11 See https://numbots.com/.
12 See https://www.topmarks.co.uk/maths-games/hit-the-button.
13 See https://www.timestables.co.uk/.

▲ Select a game – I get pairs to trial the games and feed back to the class. That way, if they get stuck, don't like it or it's not exciting enough for their little PlayStation-warped minds, knowing they have to feed back keeps them on task.

● Prodigy Math Game (free).[14] This is an interactive game and true gamification as the algorithm recognises the player's development and, hence, increases the challenge as they play. This allows an entire class to work, but work is matched to the ability level of each child and is incredibly addictive (what gamification is for). It fits into my mantra of 'little and often'. Ideally the children each have their own device and you just set it up and off they go – but colleagues have worked this in pairs, which supports discussion. As the teacher, you also receive a weekly update on play and progress. Not all 'sitting quietly doing maths' is a good thing, as I have found myself explaining to parents on more than one occasion. If you are just using this for times tables, you need to ensure that the children know not to get distracted by all the other maths areas it has on its system. We don't want the children getting ahead of us, do we?!

MAKE USE OF EARLY MORNING WORK

If you want the children to engage with these online activities at home, use early morning work to let them experiment and explore in class. Do this every now and

---

14 See https://www.prodigygame.com/main-en/.

again and you'll see the uptake at home skyrocket. Circulate and monitor what's going on in real time – and have a go yourself – and they will get the message that these apps are of real value.

SUPPORT PARENTS EFFECTIVELY

As I said at the outset, home learning can be a thorny issue for many parents, frequently based on their personal experiences or those of their older children. I have found that the best thing I can do for the children is make sure I support their parents effectively, particularly as unhomework will be a new and possibly controversial concept for them. In this way you can ensure that it becomes another area of your working life in which things become easier *and* you achieve more, all with less input.

So, when considering how you approach home learning and supporting parents, ask yourself ...

HAVE I CONSIDERED THIS FROM THEIR PERSPECTIVE?

Be understanding and consider what is *reasonable* for home learning. Yes, creating a model of the solar system might be a nice idea, but is it *reasonable* in terms of cost, effort and time? Think about those parents who will spend a fortune because they feel they have to as well as those who will feel they have to spend a fortune but don't have a fortune to spend.

Never set tasks just because you think you have to. Be clear about what it is you want to achieve from the work and how it fits into the wider scheme of learning.

ARE MY INSTRUCTIONS CLEAR?

If not, it's amazing how they will be interpreted. I would heartily suggest discussing with colleagues what your message is before sending it out – especially those who are parents (regardless of whether you are too) and particularly non-teachers.

If you make your expectations clear, make sure you then stick to them. This will support the parents as it provides surety and clarity, and can easily be referred back to, especially if you couple this with having a clear routine and provide them with examples of work.

WHAT RESOURCES CAN I PROVIDE?

Recognise that some parents, understandably, will be in a position to offer more for their children, so provide a list of easily accessible resources and sites they should use. You will be able to quality-control this list and by offering recommendations, you recognise parents' desire to support their children further, which in itself will mean a lot.

This advice is relevant for any work you expect children to undertake at home, especially research. Guiding parents regarding what reliable websites their children should use – for example, Britannica Kids,[15] BBC Teach,[16] BBC Bitesize,[17] Ducksters[18] and the likes, particularly if you have used them in school already – will be far better for everyone's nerves and patience than the overwhelming nature of a Google

15 See https://kids.britannica.com/kids.

16 See https://www.bbc.co.uk/teach.

17 See https://www.bbc.co.uk/bitesize/levels/zbr9wmn.

18 See https://www.ducksters.com.

search or the empty gesture of a Wikipedia copy and paste. This is a great opportunity to teach the children about citing sources too, getting them to include an 'Information sourced from ...' sentence at the end of their work.

HOW DO I COMMUNICATE EFFECTIVELY?

First, make sure you get your message across as often as possible and, second, ensure you are consistent. This should be done not only through your class page on the school website or via Twitter but also in person. Speaking to parents is still the best medium (however scary this may be) and if you need to phone them because they're not there at home time, just do it. Also, ensure that your written and spoken messages are the same, otherwise there are gaps to be exploited (they can smell weakness). An element of two-way communication is useful for everyone too, without, of course, ceding to every request.

AM I BEING CONSIDERATE?

Following on from the previous point, it is important to remember that the experiences parents had of their own school days will have an impact on their children, all the more so if those experiences were negative. It is important to bear this in mind – without letting go of your high expectations for every child – when supporting families whose literacy and numeracy levels are low. Knowing that the work you set may trigger and reinforce their own negative experiences will help you keep them onside from the off. Watch out too for the 'It's a whole-school expectation' attitude when confronting parents about the lack of work or effort from their child as that can be counterproductive. Avoid being draconian and heavy-handed or avoiding the potentially tricky conversation by applying this one-size-fits-all phrase as a way of trying to enforce compliance – especially as it is unlikely to work anyway. Instead, take the time to understand the individual concerns and nuances that are behind any issues with home learning. Simply telling parents (and children) that 'the school expects it' will never achieve understanding, or compassion.

A more positive approach is to make parents realise that the best home learning is unhomework and that they are already doing it anyway. If parents realise that they can have a huge influence on their child's progress without any extra effort, the pay-off is both immense and ongoing. Here are some examples of easy-win activities that parents could well already be doing with their children:

- Shopping.
- Cooking/baking.
- Cleaning/tidying.
- Going on a nature walk.
- Owning a pet.
- Bike riding.
- Having conversations while driving the car (the adult, not the child).
- Looking out of the window.
- Playing board games.
- Completing jigsaw puzzles.
- Listening to music.
- Watching TV or a film together.
- Talking to each other – especially as a result of any of the above.

What else could you add to the list? This is what I mean by 'everyday learning activities'. I won't labour the point any further, but I am sure you can easily see how literacy and numeracy skills could be included in these activities. It doesn't take much of a stretch to include other skills too.

Finally, while considering how to support parents and thinking about how to make home learning as valuable and impactful as possible, I think there is one tip that we should all consider.

WORKING SMARTER TIPS

REMEMBER LOCKDOWN

My advice for home learning is to use and extend the ideas, approaches and creativity that we were forced to develop overnight during the COVID-induced lockdowns and school closures. That toothpaste is not going back in the tube! For example, videos of explanations and worked examples can still be shared to support home learning as a helpful how-to for children and parents. Creative ways of working at home could and should be used again, including the use of marshmallows, pasta, socks and the likes for creating arrays instead of worksheets.

CHAPTER CONTEMPLATIONS

This chapter will have given you the opportunity to recognise that, irrespective of time and location, we can, should and do have a huge impact upon the learning our children experience. By rethinking playtime, lunchtime and what happens after home time we ensure that it all adds to the entirety of the child's learning experience. It takes a bit of time to set up initially, but it's an investment that pays dividends.

Take a few moments now to pause, reflect and consider your role in learning outside the classroom. Ask yourself ...

- Do I take an active or passive role at these times?

- How do I support other adults (midday supervisory assistants (MSAs)/LSAs/parents)?

- Am I guilty of buck passing and/or simply citing the school rules?

- Do I complain about things that I actually do have control over?

- Am I too worried about what colleagues might say (e.g. about eating lunch with my class)?

- How much time do post-playtime/lunchtime conversations take? (Or how long should they take if you know you're guilty of avoiding them?)

- What are the consequences, intended or otherwise, of the home learning I am setting currently?

- How effective is it at complementing the classroom-based learning?

- How good am I at communicating with parents?

- In a nutshell, do I make sure that I get the best out of my class in every way that I possibly can?

CHAPTER 4

TESTING

Unfortunately, while I would like this to be the shortest chapter in the book, we need to recognise that under current education policy thinking (or lack thereof), testing is here to stay.[1] After all, it is clear that tests are the tool that those who know least about education love most. Until the glorious day when we have a more enlightened approach to assessment, one that is fully focused on using the data to improve the children and not the other way around, let's explore how we can work smarter towards getting testing right, without the burden and stress of the process overwhelming children, teachers and parents alike.

IN-CLASS ASSESSMENT

The old adage goes that planning is important, but plans are a waste of time, and the same can be said of tests. Testing as a way of helping children to be motivated to learn and retain new information and to know how well they are performing these important skills is a proven classroom strategy. It is a great tool in your teaching toolbelt – but nothing more – so here are some tips for using that tool smartly.

---

1   I know there will be protestations, in England at least, that things have changed under Ofsted's new framework, that school data is not *as* important in an inspection and that schools are judged differently. However, having personally experienced the new framework, and from conversations with colleagues, there are still data judgements being made, even before the inspector steps foot into the school. So, beware.

WORKING SMARTER TIPS

KNOW YOUR CURRICULUM

As I said in Chapter 2, this is fundamental for success-ful teaching. Avoid teaching something just because you *think* you should be teaching it. Only teach what you should be – unless you've got this all covered and have time to teach other things, but make sure the children know what they should!

TEST FIRST

If you *know* your curriculum, you can design a test to see what the children already know and can recall, with a particular focus on what they *should* have been taught. And by test, I don't mean answering questions with pencil and paper all the time. It can be a practical exercise and include oral answers.

An example of this came last year when my Year 3 class knew that plants had male and female parts (Year 5 science) but didn't know that the stem trans-ported water around the plant (Year 2 science). Many had a vague idea about 'photo-something'. Clearly, their previous teacher had 'done plants', but the test highlighted what *I* needed to teach them. In this way, you can know, not assume.

I know that many colleagues use KWL grids for this purpose – which ask the children to note what they already know; what they want to know; and what they learned – but this also relies on the children remem-bering the teaching. What's more, the children will support each other. Aided and abetted by a teacher collating the responses, we end up with a general idea of what the class thinks it knows but no real idea of what each child *actually* knows (or doesn't). This is why a well-structured, varied test is priceless in offering you an understanding of what you need to recap and properly cement in place before you can build on it.

CALL IT WHAT IT IS BUT DON'T MAKE IT A BIG DEAL

Many teachers avoid using the word 'test' with their class. But why? If the word already has negative connotations for your class, you can work to disabuse them of these before it becomes a big thing. You can also work to embed in their thinking the definition of a 'test' that I use from the Cambridge Dictionary:

> *A way of discovering, by questions or practical activities, what someone knows, or what someone or something can do ...*[2]

In other words, a test is to see what you know, or at least what you can remember, not what you don't. And once you know what they know, you know where to start. Also, note the 'practical activities' part of the definition. I know that formal testing is often not like this, but for your purposes a test can be whatever you want it to be. So, make it multilayered and consider how you can ensure that *everyone* can share their understanding, knowledge and recall (in that order).

---

2 See https://dictionary.cambridge.org/dictionary/english/test.

'FAILURE' IS OK

One child has just scored three out of ten in a test and another has scored ten out of ten. Which one do you give the gold sticker to?

Well, for a start, it's a trick question. Don't give gold stickers. Second, both results mean that you – the teacher – have a lot to learn. Why did the child get three? Was that a good result for them? What strategies (to borrow from Carol Dweck) did they use to achieve that score, for better or for worse? What was their motivation like? Did they try (again, look to Dweck's writing on effort)? In the same way that a good doctor will look beyond the illness to find the healthy person it is hiding, what is that test result obscuring?

Meanwhile, the ten out of ten pupil may well be sending you an important message that neither of you tried hard enough, especially if such a high score is a regular occurrence. You need to design a better test that will really stretch the child beyond recall to show understanding, reasoning and practical application, for example.

For both children, obsessing about 'failure' will only make things worse. After all, if you have created a happy, safe and positive classroom environment, in which undertaking a test is *not* a big deal, then missing out on full marks is not an issue and the focus is, instead, on personal achievement, growth and development, not simply the score at the end. Otherwise, it's like saying that a striker who doesn't score 100% of their shots, or a gymnast who does not achieve a perfect score when trying a new element in a routine, or a singer who experiments with a different genre and does not get to number one are no good and failures. Madness. If the element of practice is conducted in a low-stakes manner, then performance will be tackled with a comparable mindset, making success all the more likely – especially if you have secured that nurturing environment. Similarly – and I'll admit that this is harder to achieve, especially with some parents – comparisons are not helpful either. After all, that child scoring three out of ten may have actually done better – relative to their previous performance – than the one with the perfect ten.

Given all the work that has emanated from Carol Dweck's book on mindsets, we know that we need to be building resilience and normalising failure along the way. It's about how *we* manage, support, model and deal with this other f-word that's important.

PREPARE FOR TESTS

In my experience, children work a lot harder in preparation for a test if they know what's going to be on it. When testing in class, I'm particularly fond of such phrases as:

- 'I'd remember this if I were you.'

- 'This is something that I'll ask you about later.'

- 'X, what did Y just say? This is on the test so I want everyone to know it.'

This is because in-class testing should support, and be part of, your overall teaching strategy and so – unlike other tests the children may sit – shouldn't be designed to catch them out.

IT'S NOT ALL ABOUT THE SCORES

I know that there are some teachers who create tests in which every child scores almost perfect marks. (My daughter was once in such a class!) This allowed them to conclude what a great job of teaching they must have done and, at the time, I didn't get it. However, it transpired that they felt under great pressure from their SLT, so creating tests in which everyone scored highly meant they had 'evidence' of how well things were going. That said, I'm sure (!) your school is not like this and you understand that in-class tests are there to inform your teaching and nothing more.

NOT ALL TESTS ARE
CREATED EQUAL

It's your test, so go wild. Don't just click and print. Enjoy finding new, varied and effective ways to find out what your children know and can do, and ensure that everyone has the opportunity to show off. So, when considering how you approach setting a test, ask yourself, where are:

- The drawings?

- The short answers?

- The long answers?

- The opportunities for argument and disagreement?

- The chances to speculate?

- The practical elements?

- The tick boxes?

- The cloze exercises?

- The reading opportunities and challenges?

- The persuasion elements?

- The opportunities to apply – not just regurgitate – learning and knowledge?

- The opportunities for individualism?

- The use of Lego?

This is not an exhaustive list. Please feel free to add your own elements too.

MAKE MARKING EASY

The problem with in-class tests – and the reason why so many colleagues will shy away from them – is that you then have to mark them. But, as the song goes, it ain't necessarily so. Therefore, when pondering how you approach marking tests, put your work smarty pants on and consider:

- Self-marking – using a prepared answer sheet/rubric.

- Peer marking – using a prepared answer sheet/rubric.

- Self *then* peer marking – which introduces the concept of moderation.

- Class marking – allowing for feedback as you go.

- Marking for home learning – involving the parents is good, as long as they understand the previous points about test scores and resilience.

- Galleries – peers comment on how knowledge has been applied.

- Discussion – perfect for practical forms of testing (which happens all the time in subjects like art, PE, design technology and music).

- Technology – as mentioned earlier, Google Forms allows you to set up a quiz form and identify the right answers, then does the marking for you, even producing a results spreadsheet.

Of course, these approaches still involve you, the teacher, doing a lot of the groundwork, so let's get even smarter. When considering how you approach testing, ask yourself …

WHY AM I CREATING THE TESTS IN THE FIRST PLACE?

If you show the children what you are looking for in the autumn term, then from that point on, they can create the tests instead. Here is one way of doing it:

- The class reviews what should be in a particular test.

- The class reviews and decides the types of questions they might like to use.

- You create groups then ask each group to provide questions *and* answers.

- Each group is responsible for practising to answer the questions, whereby they test them on each other, to ensure fairness and clarity, and that no one is trying to catch their peers out with nonsense.

- The questions are then swapped across the groups and the tests carried out.

Of course, as the groups are working you and your LSA can circulate and check that all is going well, with an eagle eye on spelling too, if necessary. If you have trained your class well, they will enjoy the challenge. If you haven't, the activity will degenerate into some form of intraclass pub quiz, especially if you make the mistake of allowing them to use a computer.

Done well, all the children are reviewing their learning without any significant input from you.

WHY AM I MARKING THE TESTS?

If the children have created the test, then they can mark it. Seems fair! As is so often the case, the devil is in the detail with regard to *how* this is done:

1   Create the test as per the previous example.

2   Do the test.

3   Peer-mark the test, where children from each 'side' of the room sit together and go through each set of answers.

And then comes the important bit:

4   In pairs, discuss the test and give feedback to each other.

This is where inaccuracies – and arguments – can be nipped in the bud. Yes, you will need to offer the children some up-front training, but it's all part of the learning, and has the advantage of increasing their engagement and saving you time and effort in the long run. Don't keep these benefits to yourself. When your class moves into the next year, let their new teacher know what they can do. They'll thank you for it.

TIMES TABLES

In England at least, times tables have become something of a battleground in the fight for the soul of primary education with the introduction of yet more tests. Children are expected to achieve a level of competence two years earlier than we would previously have aimed for, an example of what's known as 'academic creep'.[3]

As mentioned in relation to homework, of course times tables are important and any teacher worth their salt will have been working on them without any extra pressure from on high. But how can we be smart when it comes to times tables?

WORKING SMARTER TIPS

DON'T STRESS 'EM, EMBRACE 'EM

Accept times tables and make them part of your everyday practice. As a leader, make sure this is done across the whole school and is not just the responsibility of certain year groups, especially when there are

---

3   Insert your own joke here.

national tests involved. Start early and remember that all maths schemes of work have tables at their heart – and for good reason – so embrace them as an essential part of learning.

Across the whole school, ensure that maths learning steps aren't glossed over, skipped or ignored altogether. Each year, children should be building their understanding and mastery of skills and knowledge, including times tables. It is vital to ensure that all the relevant information is passed on during your end-of-year handover (the maths lead in your school will probably be onto this). If you don't receive it, for whatever reason, ask for it.

As you embrace the need to get times tables right with your class, here are some simple questions to consider to ensure that they don't become a burden on either time or energy.

CAN I USE TECHNOLOGY?

As ever, the effective use of technology not only saves you time but also helps with learner engagement, with gamification being a great way to stimulate interest.[4] The examples on page 101 are ideal for this and also proved effective during lockdown. That said, it is important to model, trial, explain and discuss any new apps or websites in class before they are used at home.

---

4   See https://wwwtopmarks.co.uk/maths-games/hit-the-button. It's amazing how many children like to spend their 'learning break' on these programs and don't realise it's *still* learning.

HAVE I MADE THEIR IMPORTANCE EXPLICIT TO PARENTS?

It's not the testing that's important, it's the fact that secure knowledge of times tables underpins so much of the rest of the maths curriculum that makes it invaluable to all learners. Make sure parents are playing their part; they can (and should) be part of the everyday home learning I suggested in Chapter 3. Talking of parents, encourage them to never imply that an inability to do times tables is in any way genetic! Just because they might have struggled – might still struggle – with the 7 times table, that's no excuse for suggesting that their children won't be able to do it.

CAN I BUILD TIMES TABLES INTO OTHER LESSONS?

One of the best ways to do this, in my experience, is in PE.[5] When you're playing a ball game, for example, as the children are passing, get them to count their passes using a given times table, for example 'Complete 12 passes using the 8 times table' so as each pass is made you hear, 8 – 16 – 24 – 32 – etc. Neurologically, this works well, as with the hands occupied it is the recall part of the brain that is being tested. You can also see which pairs are passing swiftly, and check that it's because of their expert recall.

Back in the classroom, you can practise times tables when you're organising the class – for example, 'There's 28 of you today, I want you in 7 groups.' You can also model using times tables, for example, when you are handing out books, by counting up in a given table as you distribute them, or getting the children to.

---

5 I trained as a PE teacher, so draw your own conclusion here.

CAN I USE THEM AS A LEARNING BREAK?

It's amazing how introducing a mid-lesson learning break can easily con children into doing more learning – especially if it's pacy and doesn't last too long. A great game for this is 'Slap it':

- In pairs, child A holds their palms facing up; child B holds their palms facing down over child A's.

- Teacher calls a table (e.g. the 6 times table).

- Child B says the first calculation (e.g. $6 \times 1 = 6$), slaps (gently) child A's hands and then they switch.

- Child A says the second calculation (e.g. $6 \times 2 = 12$), slaps (gently) child B's hands and then they switch.

- This continues until they finish the twelfth calculation.[6]

You and your LSA can simply walk around the room listening, checking that the format is being followed and that no one is simply reciting the answers instead of completing the full calculations.

Of course, you can play with the format – for example, with the children going up to 12 x the table and then coming back down again, which would mean that both children would have odd and even multipliers. Alternatively, set a time limit and challenge the children to complete as much as they can before your bell/buzzer/whistle/clap. After one round of the game, switch partners and repeat the process. I find that four rounds of 'Slap it' is usually enough, as it allows you to look at two different times tables twice, with the children working with a different partner each time. As the children become more confident, use a different table each time for four different tables.

---

6 In recent COVID-19 non-contact times, this worked just fine using 'invisible passing' instead. Once the calculation was recited, child B passed an imaginary ball to child A. It could even work in break-out rooms on Zoom, I'm sure.

Other enjoyable multiplication games that I use as learning breaks include:

- Crazy slap it. This time everyone recites the same table, working with partners in the same way, but the order is randomised and you display the calculation you want next on the board via PowerPoint or an alternative.

- Buzz. I'm sure everyone has played this game (although as a student drinking game, the details may be sketchy). Count around the circle and when you get to a number that's in the assigned times table the child says 'Buzz' instead. The voice of experience says you should, if possible, break the class into smaller circles, otherwise it can get boring and laborious if you're child 30 – especially going up to 12 x any number. This works well in table groups too.

- Groups. I *love* this game, especially as it tends to catch out the children (often boys) who like to be the cleverest *and* the quickest. Like a great mathematical Simon Says, it tests listening as well as division. It is played by the teacher saying, 'There are X of you – get into groups of Y.' If X is divisible by Y then they should get into the groups; if it's not (and there are no remainders allowed) then *no one* should move. Anyone who does is out. I play anywhere between three and seven rounds of this, enough to build some energy, but not enough to become too boring (I hope!).

CAN I USE CIRCLE TIME?

We have circle time every morning to allow the children to share how they are feeling, but this is also a great opportunity to practise times tables in a fun and non-threatening way. Copying someone else's answer is allowed but this approach can also really stretch your more able.

I choose a times table and the children have to give me facts about it as we go around the circle. For example:

Me: Today it's the turn of the 3 times table.

Child 1: 1 x 3 is 3.

Child 2: There are 6 threes in 18.

Child 3: 10 x 3 is 30.

Child 4: 100 x 3 is 300.

Child 5: There are 9 threes in 27.

Child 6: 1 x 3 is 3.

And so on ...

Please note that child 6 isn't corrected or challenged. They have either copied child 1 or chosen a simple fact, so I make a mental note to start with them next time. The only circumstance in which I do challenge or interrupt is if there's an error (I often appoint a 'tables guru' for the circle to support me in this) or a ridiculous fact (e.g. 3 x a million is 3 million – which is true, but I'd rather they concentrated on knowing that 30 divided by 3 is 10).

HOW EFFECTIVE ARE MY DISPLAYS?

There's a whole section on displays in Chapter 7, but here is some specific advice relating to times tables. Look at your classroom with fresh eyes and ask yourself: to what extent is it supporting the learning of times tables? Everyone will have their own variations on a theme – from washing lines to wall displays, displays on the door, above the interactive whiteboard or even on the tables – but let me nudge you further with the following questions:

- Is the display clear?

- Is there challenge for everyone?

- Can all the children see it? (See the section on seating in Chapter 1.)

- Where's the display of those times tables that you have already worked on?

- How are they presented – uniformly, randomly, backwards?

- Is the display missing any numbers?

- How have you used colour?

- Does your LSA understand what you want from the display?

- Is the display there for a purpose or just to look nice?

- When did you last refer to the display?

- When did you last update the display?

- When was the display last used as an *active* part of your teaching?

- When did you last see a child refer to the display?

- How have you used your displays to focus on times tables that children struggle with? (And do you know what they need more support with?)

STANDARDISED TESTS

Wherever you are working, you will probably be faced with national standardised tests.[7] While that is out of your control, the way in which you and your school approach them isn't, so do pay attention at interview and do your best to find a school where they are not the be-all and end-all, as that won't end well for anyone.

What follows are my working smarter tips for such tests.

WORKING SMARTER TIPS

RECOGNISE THAT LANGUAGE COUNTS

Choose the language you use, both in writing and orally, carefully. Preparing the children by clearly and consistently using the sort of language they will meet in the tests should start well before the tests do, even before the children enter your year. For example, make sure that you use key words that will be used in the tests not only in conversation and teaching, but also in displays and in the children's responses. The more comfortable the children become with the language used, the less scary the test becomes.

Talking of language, plan the wording of your questions well. Carefully constructed questions, using

---

7   I intend to start a campaign in England as, what with baseline tests, phonics screening, Key Stage 1 SATs, times tables tests and Key Stage 2 SATs, Years 3 and 5 are feeling left out.

higher order vocabulary, will need more planning and consideration, but will pay huge dividends in the long run. Back this up by expecting and celebrating higher order vocabulary in the verbal and written interactions your class have with you and each other. Will it help? Indubitably.

FAMILIARITY DOESN'T NEED TO BREED CONTEMPT

Rehearsal through in-class tests – without going mad about it – helps prepare children for the rigours of the test ahead. A brief, simple example would be, in maths, to ask the children to reason out why they think something, or to give two statements and ask which is correct and why. It's the reasoning that gets the mark in the test (although, for you, this offers valuable insights into the holes in their current understanding).

DON'T MAKE IT YOUR FORCE MAJEURE

Yes, you've got to do them, but the constant cry of 'It's in the test' (as in the SATs, not your in-class, testing-for-learning tests) is a sign of lazy pedagogical thinking – and not in a good way. With careful planning, consider how you can construct learning that develops cognition and reinforces the notion that learning is a good and enjoyable thing to do in and of itself, and that success is possible for all children. Oh, and it's in the test.

REMEMBER WHAT THE TEST TESTS

While I am no fan of so many national tests, it is important to remember that they exist to test the curriculum. Delivering a rich, vibrant, well-rounded curriculum and exposing your children to a wide range of reading will prepare them just as surely for a test as the constant practice papers that I am aware some schools do weekly, daily even, at certain times of the year. Which is no way to spend your childhood, surely.

READ, READ, READ

Put simply, children who have access to quality reading material at home are at an advantage in tests. There is only so much you or Dolly Parton can do about that. What you can do is make sure that you have the right books on hand in school to help every reader in your class, whatever their background.

So, when considering how you approach reading, ask yourself ...

DO I KNOW WHICH BOOKS ARE SUITABLE FOR WHICH AGE RANGE, AND WHICH WILL SUPPORT, STRETCH OR CHALLENGE?

This is a simple task and there are many resources to help. I like BookTrust, but I would also recommend visiting bookshops too. I've always found the staff knowledgeable and helpful (take that, Amazon), all the more so when I explain that I'm a teacher, after which they often recommend authors my class might like.

Helping the class know the levels is important too – and at my school we still employ a reading scheme for the children once they become free readers. This means that they can have access to high-quality texts and have their choices monitored. After completing two books from the scheme, they have a completely free choice of book, before reading another two and then repeat. This is especially important once they become free readers and are less likely to have their choices monitored.

HAVE I EXPOSED THE CHILDREN TO DIVERSE READING CHOICES?

Making sure that the children have a range of books available – including non-fiction books, picture books, magazines, newspapers and both hard- and paperbacks – whether in your class or school library is important.

A great way to expose the children to more reading material is to make book recommendations part of your classroom practice. It's simply done, plus it beats the interminable book review that too many people use simply as a link between reading and writing. Each child has an envelope on a class display and, once a book has been completed, they write a recommendation for a particular peer, highlighting the reason why they might like it, and add it to their envelope. The further pay-off is that, further down the line, there's a great discussion to be had about what the recipient thought about the book.

HAVE I MADE LINKS WITH, AND DIRECTED THE CHILDREN AND THEIR FAMILIES TO, OUR LOCAL LIBRARY?

I know that not every school is blessed with a library, through financial or space-saving considerations (though I would suggest that *if* reading were seen as a priority, a school *would* overcome both). However, what about your local library (assuming austerity hasn't done for it)? Have you been there? Have you taken your class there? Have you invited them in? They almost all have a summer holiday reading challenge, as well as activities during other school holidays. Promote them and this is an easy and effective link to make. Furthermore, local libraries may be able to provide topic boxes for your learning. Just ask and, as I always say, the worst they can say is no.

DO I LET THE CHILDREN KNOW THAT I HAVE SOME BOOKS THAT THEY'RE NOT READY FOR YET?

This is a great way to build anticipation. I always open new boxes of books in class, usually when the children are working – I know it will be a distraction! I also make a point of asking my LSA to put some away as 'I don't think anyone is ready for these yet.' Of course, this pays off when, on a given day, you suggest to a child, or a few, that you would like them to trial the new books and make a big point of the responsibility. I've never had a child let me down, yet.

My only suggestion is to make sure you put away a mix of books so that you can involve the entire class in this moment of feeling special. If you only ever do this for your 'best' readers, then the magic is lost overall. Plus, you lose the magic for that child who has never had a new book given to them (remember that new book smell and feel?). You'll be surprised by how many pupils that applies to.

DO I MAKE READING CENTRAL TO EVERYTHING I DO?

Identify with your class the range of reading they're going to do with you. Make them understand the different types and purposes of reading and make sure you plan for this, not only in lessons but through your timetabling:

● Reading for purpose – reading is linked to the learning.

● Reading for development – the texts are structured so as to be challenging for the children to improve their reading ability.

● Reading for pleasure – so that the children can read their own choice of texts. It is easy to mistake reading for pleasure with reading for development, which can then alienate the children.

● Reading for comprehension – working on developing specific skills identified within the curriculum.

● Reading as a class – enjoying the same book simultaneously, which also offers the children opportunities to read aloud.

● Reading to them – my class hear me read *every day*. Sometimes this might be from the class reader, but more often it is from a book that I have chosen to read to them.

AM I PREPARED TO BAN BOOKS?

I don't want to name names here (if you know, you know). Certain books, by certain celebs, may offer a bit of light relief but shouldn't be the main element of the children's reading diet. Banning books can be a thorny topic with parents, I know – more on which later.

DO I INTEGRATE READING COMPREHENSION EXERCISES INTO ALL AREAS OF THE CURRICULUM?

Not only is this great test preparation, but it's also great preparation for life. After all, what would the world be like if people didn't think deeply about and question, what they read?

DO I TELL THE CHILDREN WHAT I AM READING?

Or, better still, show them? Having genuine 'everyone reads in class' time is vital and the children (and the LSA) always like to see what I'm reading, which leads to some great conversations. I also make sure that I am modelling a wide range of reading materials.[8]

DO I READ TO THE CHILDREN?

More than just reading aloud to them, you should be modelling what a good reader does and how a good reader thinks. There is more to being a good reader than just reading the words on the page after all.

For example, I have a display that lists the qualities and behaviours of great readers, which we keep adding to over time. The children will tend to focus on pace, tone and expression, for example, but rarely ask questions or predict what will happen – which is also part of the curriculum. Asking questions or inviting reflections, such as the following, teaches them skills that we might take for granted:

● 'I wonder what will happen next.'

● 'If that doesn't happen, I wonder what could happen instead.'

● 'I wonder if they have remembered ...'

● 'But if they do X, won't Y happen?'

---

8   Books about Elvis. Magazines about Elvis. Newspaper articles about Elvis. Elvis LP sleeve notes. The full gamut.

And then follow up with phrases such as:

- 'I suppose they could ...'
- 'Or perhaps ...'
- 'Maybe ...'
- 'Then again ...'
- 'I can't wait to see.'

You can invite contributions from the class or just muse out loud for yourself as a modelling exercise (they'll do it in their heads anyway).

HAVE I GOT THE PARENTS ONSIDE?

As with homework, reading can be a Goldilocks issue, often compounded by the parents' own literacy levels and reading experiences. Taking the time to explain the importance of reading, the school's vision for it, and the role everyone (teacher, child, parent) has in it is invaluable.

Taking up an earlier point, you may well need to explain to parents why you have banned certain books and deal with the 'It's the only thing they read' or 'But if they enjoy it, what's the problem?' arguments. I tend to keep with the diet metaphor, highlighting that, given the chance, children would eat sweets as often as they could, but, as adults, we make the decision that this is not healthy for them and ensure that they have a varied diet instead, with the occasional sweet treat. It's the same with reading.

Also, remember that reading isn't a box-ticking exercise, so don't make the process of getting children to read at home overly burdensome. This was something I learned at the start of my primary teaching career when a parent asked to see me one day before school. She began by saying: 'I'm sorry! Jack didn't bring his book home last night so we couldn't do his reading. It's my fault.'

I reassured her that, as Jack was in Year 4, not taking his book home was Jack's fault, not hers, but what she said next has stayed with me ever since and helped me realise that school systems need to be realistic for parents too.

'Actually, to be honest, *I* told him not to bring the book home.'

Surprised and a bit annoyed, I asked why she would do that, and she replied: 'I knew we wouldn't have time to do everything that's needed. The new system the school has introduced is killing me. There are just not enough hours in the day. I have three other children to support with their homework, as well as various clubs, dinner, some family time and the bedtime routines to fit in all before 8pm when my eldest gets to bed.'

My affronted teacher stance began to soften, and she went on: 'The school's expectation of ten minutes of the adult reading, ten minutes of the child reading and then ten minutes of discussing the book using the questions we were sent is bad enough, but then I have to help them to look up words they don't understand and, to cap it all, you ask them to write out the words in sentences of their own!'

Her last sentence finished off both me and my strict adherence to the school rules completely: 'The night before last I got my eldest into bed, opened a bottle of wine and just sat and cried. I felt like a failure.'

Her tears flowed again at this point and her words still haunt me. The school's good intentions were making her life a misery. And she hadn't even pointed out the added lunacy of the reading record we asked parents to complete, in which they had to:

1   Comment on the child's reading (against prescribed criteria).

2   Make a note of the tricky words.

3   Write down the questions they had asked their child.

4   Record the child's responses.

I, like all the teachers at this school, was then expected to respond and repeat the process when I listened to the child read in class. This looked great on paper – or during an inspection – but was frankly dangerous in the real world.

Consider for yourself what reading system you're using and ask yourself whether it is both effective *and* realistic for all concerned. We would all do well to apply the rule that new doctors learn to any home learning tasks we set: 'First, do no harm.'

To help strike the right balance and ensure that parents can and do support the all-important reading development process, ask yourself ...

HAVE I REMEMBERED AND UNDERSTOOD THAT HOME READING IS JUST ONE PART OF A BIGGER PICTURE?

Hopefully you have a clear system in place as a school, but if you are introducing any changes in reading practice for your class, or, indeed, you have the authority to implement a whole new system, be sure to involve parents in designing it, or at least get a few of them to road test it first, and then pilot it with some classes before it is spread across the whole school. The people designing it might be parents themselves but that doesn't mean it is achievable by all parents. Reread the words of Jack's mum if you're not convinced and remember that avoiding harm is your starting point.

HAVE I COMMUNICATED THINGS CLEARLY?

I find that a face-to-face meeting is often best; however, tapping into the technology we have all become so used to, you could and probably should send out a video so that every parent is up to date with the plans and can also refer back to them. Film yourself reading with a few children too so the parents have a model of what the process might look like.

HAVE I BEEN EXPLICIT ABOUT THE ROLE THE PARENTS HAVE TO PLAY?

You want parents to be fully onside in raising expectations, not just going through a checklist of things that you have asked them to do. You can make their lives easier by directing them to quality, age-appropriate books, or, better yet, offer a class lending library, highlighting the reading progression system you have in place. Feeling that they will be reading Biff, Chip and Kipper with their child until the end of time has done for many a parent's commitment to home reading.

HAVE I MADE LINKS WITH LOCAL LIBRARIES AND PROMOTED THEM TO PARENTS?

It's amazing how many parents seem to feel that they and their children have outgrown their local library. They may have gone there to attend social parent and baby groups but stopped going once their children were a bit older. This doesn't have to be the case, though, so do remind them of the benefits of library visits and help them rekindle that love *they* had for their local library too.

HAVE I EVER INVITED PARENTS IN TO SEE HOW I RUN READING SESSIONS?

Remember, home reading is part of a bigger picture, so show them the whole and help them see how their part fits into the overall jigsaw.

HAVE I SOUGHT OUT PARENTS (OR, INDEED, OTHER FAMILY MEMBERS) TO VOLUNTEER AS READERS OR LISTENERS IN SCHOOL?

There are never enough adults in school to listen to every child read – we know that, and that's why we end up targeting adult reading time at certain children. But what about seeing if parents are able to help? When I was a child at primary school – back in the 1970s and 1980s, before LSAs – this was how classroom support was provided. The safeguarding protocols are more onerous these days, of course, but it's definitely worth doing in the long run.

HAVE I MADE SURE I PRAISE THEM ON THE GREAT JOB THEY ARE DOING AS THEIR CHILDREN MOVE UP THE READING SCHEME?

Make sure a child's progress is cause for joint celebration and acknowledge that the parent will undoubtedly have worked hard too.[9] I've also found that those who haven't done their bit (and some will openly admit to that) will be

---

9   The Biff, Chip and Kipper Magic Key award for perseverance comes to mind here.

inspired to get more involved if they know these efforts are being noted.

HAVE I MADE CLEAR MY VIEWS ON WHAT READING IS AND ISN'T?

There's more to reading than just saying the words on the page. The act of reading involves understanding, inferring, predicting, summarising, making links, spotting references and more. This is why parents need to see it modelled by a professional. Again, invite them in or create a video so that they can see – and revisit – your expectations.

HAVE I PREPARED MYSELF FOR THE WORST?

Some parents just can't – or won't – do it. It's as simple as that. You will just have to double down on your efforts with their child in school. Equally, don't be bullied by parents who judge their child to be better at reading than you do. I heard one Year 2 parent proclaiming to a teacher that their child had 'read Harry Potter', when in actual fact the child knew a few words and had seen the film. You're the professional here, so be open but resolute.

CHAPTER CONTEMPLATIONS

This chapter has been all about testing (and reading, which helps with testing) and, despite still lamenting the way in which we over-test in an education system that runs on data milked from children, I hope you better understand the role that testing plays in children's learning.

When considering your approach to testing, ask yourself:

● How important are the tests to me *really*?

● Do I remember that tests are everyone's responsibility?

● Knowing this, do I support my colleagues with *their* testing?

● What role do the children play in their tests?

● How effective am I at using the time I have?

● Can I communicate more effectively with my class' parents?

● How effectively do I use language?

And, for me, the most important consideration of all:

● What is the true environment and culture of the school as evidenced by the school's approach to testing?

This last question is fundamental for me. When the actions of your school's leadership, if not the words, make test results the be-all and the end-all of school life, then everyone's mental health will be affected, year after year. The top-down pressure on you can also lead to moral and ethical dilemmas that can impact on your professional judgement.[10]

So, choose your school carefully and use testing for good.

---

10 And, yes, I have had a head teacher who expected me to very subtly cheat in SATs – with a surreptitious nod here, cough there and tap of the finger as I walked past a desk – causing me to leave that school. This was compounded by the justification that 'Everyone else is doing it.' What's more, I know that this is not an isolated incident, such is the pressure of high-stakes data-led accountability on people who started off wanting to make a difference and ended up making a mess of things.

CHAPTER 5

TRANSITION

The challenges of transition during the pandemic meant that teachers will have missed out on all the things that make that move from one class, key stage or school to another infuriating and insightful in equal measure. You know what I mean!

- The child who doesn't shut up all day.

- The child who asks you inappropriate questions (e.g. 'How old are you, Mr Creasy?').

- The child who gets upset because you've rearranged the room.

- The child who gets upset because you sit them away from their friend.

- The child who asks the same question as someone else, that's been answered three times already.

- The child who hangs around at play- or lunchtime not wanting to go out.

- The child, usually children, who are late or early.

- Not forgetting, of course, the attitude of the parents at pick-up towards you and their child. The ones who don't even look up from their mobile phone to acknowledge you, let alone their child. Or the ones who want to relive everything from the past year.

All of these moments help you start to form a picture of the class you will be inheriting, and, in my experience, are incredibly instructive for the year ahead. I certainly missed them during COVID-related school closures. Assuming that things are at least closer to normal by the time you read this, what follows are my working smarter tips to make transition as smooth and effective as possible. In writing them, I recognise that every school will have procedures and protocols in place, but these pointers are for you – the class teacher – to make your life easier.

To kick off, here are two important general principles to remember, regardless of the type of transition or time of year.

WORKING SMARTER TIPS

MAKE THEM FEEL SPECIAL, REGARDLESS

Whether you are waving a tearful goodbye to a class or greeting your new class with an animated sense of anticipation, whether your tears are in gratitude for not having to deal with the class from hell any more or your anticipation is tinged with foreboding as that difficult cohort has finally reached you, the rule still applies: make them feel special.[1]

For the class on their way out of your door for the last time, make sure that they know how much you love them, what a joy it was to teach them and that you recognise them as *individuals* – not just as part of a homogenous lump called 5C or whatever. Much of this, of course, will be conveyed in your end-of-year report (if not, why not?) but make sure you take the

---

1 As is so often the case, especially if you are a new teacher, the 'fake it till you make it' approach will stand you in good stead here.

time to speak to each child individually before they leave.

For the class on their way in, make sure they know how excited you are to be teaching them, the positive things you've heard about them (ignore the negatives and make up your own mind) and what exciting learning adventures you will have together in the coming year.

NEVER MAKE LIGHT OF THE CHANGE

Never underestimate the magnitude and impact of transition on any child, including the most confident ones. Be even more mindful of the child transitioning in isolation for whatever reason.

A joke is not always the best place to start. You might think, 'I asked for the ugliest class this year and, lo and behold, here you are!'[2] is just the banter you need to set the year off to a great start, but I'd suggest you are actually making things worse for everyone.[3] Banter – the good sort – has its uses, but the priority here is to make the children feel safe, loved and wanted. And, yes, I have used the l-word here. In over 25 years of teaching, I've enjoyed working with every class I've taught, but while I have only truly loved a few (five immediately spring to mind), every class *felt* loved, I assure you.

---

2 True story.

3 Imagine your words, taken out of context, relayed without emotion or nuance to the parents at home that evening. Then choose your words carefully.

ANNUAL TRANSITION

This usually happens as one academic year draws to an end and the groundwork is being laid for the next. I will assume that you will be on the receiving end of a brand-new class but much of what follows also applies if you are keeping the same class into the following year.

WORKING SMARTER TIPS

START BEFORE THE START

You will (should!) know which class you are receiving next year before the children and parents do, so use this time to observe them. If you are in a leadership role, this can be done in class (with your colleague's agreement) under the entirely plausible guise of a lesson observation. If you are not a leader, make the most of the times you can see them around the school – break, lunch, assembly, the start or end of the day, out of your classroom window (something you can also do if you are a leader). Careful observations at these incidental times will yield invaluable insights into how they operate, their characteristics, their friendship – or otherwise – groups and how they interact with others.

Use my advice from Chapter 3 and employ playtimes and lunchtimes to sit and chat with them, getting to know them beyond their learning. In this way I have been able to find out, in advance, who are the children who will 'manage' the allocation of players in teams so that they never lose, who is on the periphery, who is the wind-up expert who then stands back innocently when there's an explosion, who looks out for others, who excludes, who is excluded and much more.

TALK ISN'T CHEAP

Your colleague – their current teacher – is a mine of information about the class, in particular the nuances that won't get recorded in any handover documentation (see Appendix 2 for an example of this). It might sound obvious, but before transition day talk to them as much as possible and find out about the class (keeping an open mind regarding any negatives you hear). Make sure that you invest time in speaking to the other adults who work with the children too. This is vital as they'll have a different insight into the class plus, as many LSAs move with their classes, a longitudinal angle to share too.

FIND OUT WHAT WORKS

It would be the height of arrogance to ignore the wisdom of your new class' previous teacher. They will (hopefully) have worked out how to make the class tick, and this information will allow you to hit the ground running. What is also useful is for them to share the class conundrums they didn't solve, as this can be an invaluable source of insight.

As the receiving teacher, I recommend that you take on board this knowledge, especially if you are new to the school. After all, the children will soon let you know if you're not following school procedure in the right way. This doesn't mean that you should try to recreate yourself in their former teacher's image, but, to weigh it with 'being yourself' and to be aware how the change of teacher can affect children.

KNOW WHAT WORKS, THEN BE PREPARED TO CHALLENGE OR CHANGE IT

As we've established, you're not trying to imitate the class' former teacher, nor are you trying to outdo them. When you do get the low-down on your new class from their former teacher, I advise considering the following caveats:

- You aren't them.

- They aren't you.

- The children will have changed and grown.

- Your job isn't to let them settle back into a zone of comfort or mediocrity.

When having these conversations with the previous teacher, be ready to listen to and take on board, but also to reframe, the comments you may hear. This is a challenge I enjoy every year. For example:

Comment	Insight
'They don't like working in groups.'	They will have to work in a group, with a specific focus, potentially with allocated roles, but definitely with a clear structure, purpose and success criteria.

Comment	Insight
'He won't work with girls.'	He will be seated with and will have to work with girls, but will be paired with the most empathetic and supportive ones (and the same will go for his friends to avoid any teasing or him feeling unduly singled out).
'She used to like maths, and she is good at it, but I think the boys' attitudes and competitive-ness have put her off.'	I will try to restore that love. For example, I find that tasks in which there are many answers, not just one, help. It's not about being fastest but about the quality of the answer.
'They hate to lose – I always engineer it so they don't. It's not worth the hassle when they do.'	I'll ensure that games are played which means they will lose, or at least not always win.
'They work really well with their friends, but no one else. Hates it if someone else is paired with X [their best friend].'	I'll ensure that they do work with others, enjoy success and that their friend is similarly successful with their alternative partner. Do not have this as the only way of working, but also don't shy away from the separation. This process can be supported by creating a 'snowball', meaning the two friends can come together as part of a group of four, after first thinking their ideas through on their own and then discussing them with a partner.

Comment	Insight
'He cannot wait his turn. If his hand goes up, ask him immediately, otherwise he'll just call out or have an outburst.'	I ignore calling out, only taking responses from pupils with their hands up. This can be supported by parking questions, so that the children know who you will ask and in what order. This allows you to include the child who calls out but, bit by bit, you move them down the order of responding.
'You'll never get that one reading. They always stare out of the window, fidget, wander, do anything but read.'	I make it my mission to find out what the block is. What is it that they *do* enjoy reading? What changes can I make to help them be more comfortable in their reading? This starts with the one-to-one reading they do with me or my LSA on a daily or weekly basis. I ensure they read, even if this means starting with a sentence. That's still a win and something you can build on. I also ensure the child is never spotlighted in class, instead giving them time to read their section in advance so they are prepared.

REALLY START ON TRANSITION DAY

If you are aware of various differences in approach between you and their previous teacher, introduce these differences as soon as possible (although not all at once). What makes you different? How do you want to introduce yourself as their new teacher? I believe that you should address this on the first day you officially meet them.

For example, I always use Thunks in my teaching,[4] invariably to start the day, but also as provocations for learning and as learning breaks (which is nonsense, of course, as Thunks *are* learning and require deep thinking and reasoning). Therefore, on transition day, I will always ensure that we do some 'thunking' so that the children experience this way of working from the off. I also like playing a game of 'Would you rather?', in which everyone moves to one side of the room or the other to show their preference based on a question (no fence-sitters allowed in the middle of the classroom!). Examples I have used include:

● Would you rather eat a hot dog or a burger at a BBQ?

● Would you rather have carrots for fingers or toes?

● Would you rather go forward or backward in time?

This encourages intellectual exploration and allows me to see who copies, who bosses the others around, who moves immediately and then changes their mind, who dithers and who is desperate to find the 'right' answer (i.e. what I think).

---

4   If you're lucky enough to teach your new class during an interview, I strongly recommend using Thunks. Apart from drawing gasps of amazement from the interviewers, they give you a real insight into what to expect of the children – and what they can expect of you. See I. Gilbert, *The Little Book of Thunks: 260 Questions to Make Your Brain Go Ouch!* (Carmarthen: Crown House Publishing, 2007); and I. Gilbert, *The Compleat Thunks Book* (Carmarthen: Independent Thinking Press, 2017).

KEY STAGE 1 TO KEY STAGE 2 TRANSITION

First and foremost, the working smarter tips we've discussed in relation to annual transition still apply. That said, I think there are a few extra things to remember for a key stage transition, particularly if the move from Key Stage 1 to Key Stage 2 also involves a school move.

WORKING SMARTER TIPS

KNOW WHO THEY ARE

This tip is simple enough, but always remember, whoever they are, they are children; they aren't a data point, based on their test scores. (Use my simplified handover document in Appendix 2 to help with this. It deliberately omits data scores.) Get to know the *real* child and do your best to avoid talk of age-related expectations and the likes, whatever your SLT might say.

I recognise that, in some schools, this is going to be hard to do and I feel sorry for Year 3 colleagues – and I have been there myself – who are constantly informed about children being 'on track' or otherwise. This is usually coupled with the expectation that they'll be on track by the end of the year. Bear in mind that children who aren't on track in Key Stage 1 do actually have another four years to get back on it. The next official measurement is in Year 6, so consider Key Stage 2 as a step in what is a much bigger journey.

Regardless of the year or phase you teach, use your new start as an opportunity to unshackle children from the chains of their former achievements and misdemeanours. They shouldn't be held down like some primary-age Marley's ghost. Instead, by knowing what they don't know or can't do, you can help fill the gaps in a personal and focused way. Imagine trying to cross a river using stepping stones but some of the stones are missing. You can't progress without filling in the gaps. Big jumps usually ends in tears and a big splash, so knowing what and where the gaps are is the first step in the process.

Furthermore, ensure that parents are aware of *their* responsibilities in this process and that you intend to work in partnership with them in the best interests of their child. Let them know what you're planning to address and how they can help (and be prepared to challenge them if needed). For example, I've met many parents who are worried because their child has not met age-related expectation in reading, but they don't listen to their child read or read to them. Find out what the barriers are and see how you can help them to help you to help their child.

STEP UP INCREMENTALLY

I feel that this is especially applicable to children in Year 3, who are often still far more equipped for Key Stage 1 than they are Key Stage 2 – however mature or able they may appear (the same applies to secondary transition).

Avoid the whole 'we're doing proper teaching now' conversation. There's no need to make the learning more formal, not to mention how this sentiment is rather disrespectful to your colleagues in Key Stage 1. And never, heaven forbid, get into the 'this will be in the SATs' talk, which is simply counterproductive.

Instead, once you have spoken to your Year 2 colleague, just bear in mind the following:

- Know how to support the children.

- Understand the scaffolds needed for learning.

- Learn to be patient.

- Prepare resources and manipulatives.

- Remember, Key Stage 2 is a marathon, not a sprint.

REMEMBER THAT A RISING TIDE RAISES ALL SHIPS

Regardless of what the children in your class have achieved in the past, start the year as you mean to go on. Have high expectations for *everyone* in your class, irrespective of their age-relatedness, and ensure you exhibit this in *every* way possible: how you conduct yourself, the language you use, and how you ingrain a standard of excellence from the off. Your habits will become their habits, so make them good ones.

SECONDARY TRANSITION

'You can't compare where your child is now with the Year 6 levels. They were from primary school and what is on his report are secondary levels,' said the secondary teacher to the parent of a Year 7 child.

'I'm a primary school deputy head!' retorted the parent.

'Well, you know *exactly* what I mean,' replied the secondary teacher.

Although I am a primary teacher now, I have also been a secondary school teacher and a transition coordinator. I had to have a word with the teacher involved in this conversation, and I guess it is not an isolated incident and it, or something like it, happens in schools across the country.

The 'We're doing things properly now' mentality can happen in so many subjects (MFL teachers, I'm looking at you) but it doesn't have to be this way and there is much that primary schools can do to improve the transition process.

WORKING SMARTER TIPS

IT'S NOT ALL ABOUT SATs/ENTRANCE EXAMS/ END-OF-KEY-STAGE TESTS

If the children's last year in primary school is all about the tests they will face at the end of the summer term, then you are doing them – and yourself – a huge disservice. Make sure they leave your care as well-rounded learners, having had a range of experiences through-out Key Stage 2 and especially in Year 6 (and not just in those brief few weeks after SATs).

THE EARLY BIRD CATCHES THE WORM

While many secondaries won't really look at transition until their current Year 11 cohort head off on study leave, could you be helpful here? If you've built a relationship with the school, or, even better, want to forge one, why not get hold of the transition paperwork once the secondary allocation has been made in March? Complete your paperwork then to get ahead of the game. This is especially helpful in secondaries with a designated head of Year 7.

Yes, sometimes you may feel that you are completing the same form in different guises for every secondary school you feed into and, yes, of course it would be easier if there were just one standard form. However, when it comes to returning the information a second-ary school requires, do it quickly and understand that while you have 30 or so children to do this for, they are likely dealing with 180 or more. Plus they need to assimilate all the information to be able to organise pastoral and academic demands, including setting and, often, language choices. Remember, you're not doing it for you; it's for the benefit of the children in order to give them the best possible start at their new school. Transition is enough of a challenge as it is, especially as, to begin with, Key Stage 3 will feel like a big leap up from Key Stage 2.

When considering how you approach secondary transfer, ask yourself: what can I do? I would recommend that you work with your school to establish strong links with all the secondary schools your pupils will be joining, especially the main one your school feeds into. Take time to build connections and find out how you can help.

When it comes to preparing your class for the different styles of teaching and different way of school life they will face, you can lead them in gently in a number of ways. You could:

- Have other teachers teach them. Having a range of teachers (of different abilities and approaches) teach them is good preparation for secondary school life and has benefits for your colleagues too in terms of honing their practice. This could be as simple as swapping classes with your partner teacher or subject leader.

- Have the children leave and re-enter the classroom to signify transition between subjects. This might be seen as time wasting but it familiarises the children with compartmentalised hour-long lessons. It will sharpen your timekeeping too.

- Impose clear lesson transitions, not allowing them to blur into one another (a common – reasonable – complaint from secondary colleagues). Make sure that you offer clear timings and stick to them. If they have not been prepared, it can be a bit of a shock when a child suddenly discovers that the phrase 'You have ten minutes for this' actually means just that.

- Ensure that the children are becoming more independent (e.g. they find the equipment they need, not you or your LSA). You might do this already, but speak to your secondary colleagues about what they expect in terms of, for example, equipment. We all know our classroom 'wanderers', but this behaviour is usually not expected, let alone accepted, in secondary school. The children will need to be prepared and should have their equipment with them at all times. Why not start the day by informing your class of the day's timetable and giving them time to get their equipment ready? Alternatively, try to build good habits and routines by getting them to prepare the day before, reminding them that bag preparation is best done the night before, not the morning of!

- Encourage parents to support you in helping build their children's independence.

  A simple example here is not allowing parents to give excuses, like 'I'm sorry they haven't ... it's because I ...' Similarly, I am still astounded that some parents resemble Nepalese Sherpas at the end of school, taking all the bags and coats while their offspring dawdles along, sometimes engrossed in technology, oblivious. Make sure you address this and help make independence a cause for pride.

- Visit the secondary school and spend a day there, and/ or invite a secondary colleague to your school for the day. I previously established this as an annual 'twinning exercise' and it paid huge dividends for the schools and the children. Be prepared to go to the secondary school and see how they do things regardless of whether or not they come to the primary (you know how busy and important secondary colleagues are). As it is with parents, unless we experience school as it is now, we end up drawing on our own experiences and things may be very different these days.

- Alternatively, why not ensure that you are invited to visit the secondary school for any events they have (e.g. the GCSE art open evening or their school show). This shows support for the school but allows you to see your former pupils, something they (usually) love. Similarly, make sure that you invite the secondary school to your end-of-year play, sports day or leavers' events. You'll be surprised by how many accept – often with the line 'We've never been invited to one of these before.'

● Make subject links with your secondary school. Often, though not always, subject leaders in primary schools are not experts in their subject but do have an interest in or passion for it. Making links with the local secondary would support both parties, especially in science and design technology where there's the opportunity to go and use their specialist equipment. Possibly the best example of sharing resources was when the secondary school I worked in needed a part-time languages teacher. With some collaboration and creative thinking, we made a joint appointment in partnership with two local primaries to create a full-time position. The new member of staff delivered lessons at all three schools, which facilitated planning time and provided CPD for primary colleagues.

MID-YEAR MOVE *INTO* YOUR CLASS

I once met a child who was on a tour of the school on a Friday and was then told that they were starting in my class the next Monday, with no more information than that. Thankfully I'm not at that school now and, hopefully, your school is more enlightened, but when considering how you approach a child transferring into your class mid-year, ask yourself ...

COULD I DO A HOME VISIT?

These are common in EYFS but are also invaluable whatever the age of the child, and I would recommend doing them for every new member of your class. This means that you will meet the parents and child on their terms, so you're more likely to get to know the child better, as well as gain an invaluable insight into their family life. Again, I'd recommend the form in Appendix 2 as a starting point.

WHO LEADS THE SCHOOL TOUR?

If you lead it yourself this is a non-threatening way to meet the parents and child and you can talk a lot easier if you are showing them around the school. So, if possible, don't leave this task to a member of the office staff or SLT. Not only can you talk about learning and elicit the information you need, but you can also see how the family interacts – for example, who answers when you ask the child a question?

Alternatively, get one of your pupils to lead the tour. It may well unpick the lock and help the child open up. It's always amazing to me how often children are talked about – and over – by the adults. In my experience, a child-led tour means that there is far more interaction for the new child. This works even better if the parents don't go on the tour and spend time with the head, a member of the SLT or the new teacher instead.

WILL THE CHILD SPEND TIME WITH THEIR NEW CLASS?

On the day of the visit, allow some time in class for the child. Sadly, not all schools seem to do this (some even conduct tours after school, when no other children are there), but I have seen how useful it is for a new child to come into the class and undertake an activity. Again, Thunks are invaluable here as a low-pressure, non-threatening way for all parties to check each other out.

DO I KNOW WHAT THEY HAVE LEARNED?

This is really important as it is possible – for example, in history and with reading – that a child will have already studied something you have yet to cover. Don't see this as a burden, or as an opportunity for you to demonstrate how much better than their previous teacher you are. Allow the child to shine – can they be an expert? Can they teach your class and can you stretch their knowledge deeper? Or can you get them to examine their prior learning by thinking differently?

HAVE I SPOKEN TO THEIR PREVIOUS TEACHER?

This is simple, but effective. Make time to call their previous teacher and have a chat. You'll get all the official information you need, as well as – done well – plenty of 'unofficial' information that might prove invaluable too.

MID-YEAR MOVE *FROM* YOUR CLASS

I am not alone in suddenly being told that the following day will be the last in my class for a particular child. However, in most cases we do have more time to plan and prepare for a departure. Think about the tips in the previous section but also ask yourself: what else could I do to help? Examples include:

- Give the child time to create something to share with their new teacher or class to allow them to introduce themselves. They could share their favourite things, their hobbies, their strengths and the likes. This could be done through a presentation, a shield, a shoebox, or any of the sorts of activities you use on transition day or at the start of September.

- Speak to the child's new teacher. They might not do what I have suggested and contact you, so make time to call the receiving teacher and speak to them. Allow the child to have a proper transition. Yes, you're busy, but wouldn't you like it if someone did this for you?

- Make the child's departure special. True, your school may have a huge turnover of children, but never let a child leave without *at least* a card, made and signed by the entire class.

CHAPTER CONTEMPLATIONS

This chapter has been all about transitions and how to not only make the best of them, but to use them to enhance the school life of all concerned – including you. Transition of any kind can be a traumatic experience for a child and our job is to make such a move as smooth and painless as possible.

I appreciate that different schools will have different rates of transfer and that, for some, it may be a serene experience that occurs only once a year. Others may have more turmoil and turnover throughout the year, with classes almost completely changed in complexion and character from the start of the academic year to the end.

Either way, take the time to consider what you do – and what you could do – when it comes to transition. Investing time and effort now will save time and effort further down the line. I recognise that some of the elements of transition will be out of your hands as they may be structurally or systemically dictated; however, think about your role in the transition process and, reflecting on the general principles established throughout this chapter, ask yourself ...

- Do I support *every* child to the best of my ability?
- Do I show the children that I am bothered?
- Am I bothered?
- Do I make an effort?
- Do I support my colleagues by completing the necessary paperwork?
- Do I take the time to learn and gain insights from all colleagues, not just teachers?
- Do I try to get to know the child, looking beyond the data?
- Have I looked at any research about the impact of pupil mobility on attainment?

● Have I spotted areas where things could be improved and acted accordingly?

● Have I tried to make links with the other schools involved in transition?

And, for me, the most important consideration of all:

● If it was my child transitioning into or out of my class, would I be happy with the level of support that they received?

CHAPTER 6

WORKING WITH ADULTS

With the exception of understanding children's neurological development, this is the part of the job that is the most ignored in my experience. At interview, we will be full of our passion to spread joy, wonderment and curiosity among children everywhere, but we are rarely – if ever – asked about working with adults. Leadership interviews are different, but by then we will have already been working with other adults, for better or for worse, for a few years. However, this is a vitally important part of the job and your success – not to mention stress levels – will frequently depend on your skills in this area.

We'll come to parents and the importance of that relationship in Chapter 7 (skip ahead if you have a pressing need), but in this chapter I'm focusing on the adults with whom you share a photocopier or car park. Like the children, they will all present their own unique challenges and, just like the children, it is important to be true to yourself when dealing with them. And, as in all relationships, the secret is investing the time to make them work for all concerned – easier said than done, I know, so let's be smart about it.

To help, I've tried to consider different colleagues in clusters, with advice for each. Before we get onto this, let me share two working smarter tips that were offered to me in my first few days of teaching and that have proved invaluable throughout my teaching career (thank you Daryll Chapman, you lifesaver you!). I've also added a third of my own. These will serve you well, and I say that as someone who has seen the impact on those who did not take the advice.

WORKING SMARTER TIPS

ABOVE ALL ELSE, THE SITE MANAGER IS KING

Throughout my career, I have witnessed too many colleagues treat site managers with disdain and only deign to speak to them when they want help with one or more of the following:

● Vomit.

● Flooded toilets.

● Heavy items which need moving.

● Classroom furniture rearrangement.

● Parents' evening set-up.

● Staging for plays.[1]

Which is to say nothing of the expectations we place on them when we want to work a bit later, get in earlier, work during the holidays, forget our keys, have car trouble or need children transporting to sports fixtures, concerts and the likes (they can usually drive the minibus too). On a personal note, it's always good to have another male to talk to in a primary school – and site managers are usually male – but their gender is

---

1   Occasionally, more than one of these will occur simultaneously.

irrelevant. Please remember that site managers are not *just* there for the nasty things in life.

They have their set roles and responsibilities and any-thing above and beyond that entails asking a favour and needs to be treated with due care and considera-tion. Especially if the task is one that involves bodily fluids. If you interact with the site manager in a posi-tive and professional manner throughout the year, you are more likely to be treated favourably when you are in need. People often marvel at the fact that I get things done quickly, obligingly and usually really con-veniently. For example, any deliveries for me will be unpacked and helpfully placed in my room, rather than the box dumped for me to sort. Why? Because I take the time throughout the year.

Of course, if the site manager is king, you need to remember ...

THE OFFICE STAFF ARE QUEENS[2]

And you don't mess with them. They are often your first line of defence when it comes to irate, demanding or unreasonable parents. Like the triage nurse in A&E, they are invaluable at appropriately directing issues as soon as they come through the door, but all too fre-quently they can be undervalued and unrecognised.

Unlike the site manager, office staff may well be involved in more conversations with the teaching staff

---

2 I've never worked in a school in which the site manager is female and the office staff are male, but if that's your school, then great. Well done for breaking down gender stereotypes and please crown them all appropriately.

as they enter and exit the building past the main reception, but do they get more than this transient acknowledgement? I've yet to meet a member of office staff who *only* fulfils their job description. Their knowledge of families, individual situations and often the wider community is frequently second to none.

Remember, office staff usually:

- Live locally.

- Are (or have been) parents of children at the school.

- Have worked there for longer than many of the teaching staff have – or will.

- Have built a rapport with parents over time.

- Are well known by parents.

Making time to talk with office staff is always worth it. It also means you find out things that aren't ever written in handover documents.

Investing time means more than gifting chocolates at Christmas or inviting them to the staff do for the entertainment value (they are often better at letting their hair down than teachers, in my experience). I'm talking about real, personal investment and being genuinely bothered. It's amazing the help you get following this level of interaction, especially if, like me, you sometimes end up needing something done at the last minute. They certainly came into their own during lockdown, supporting parents who 'couldn't log on' to online lessons (shorthand for 'didn't follow the step-by-step instructions they were given') and dealing with a whole new world of requests and dilemmas. This in turn allowed me to focus on the new approach to learning that I was having to get my head around. And this was all the more impressive when they were working from home, supporting their own children with their learning.

THE CLEANERS ARE PART OF THE EXTENDED ROYAL FAMILY

You can guess what I'll say here, but I'll say it anyway. Simply put:

- Talk to your cleaner – it's usually the same person every day.

- Get to know their name – I'm always amazed at how few teachers do this.

- Find out about *them*.

- Don't make their job harder.[3]

- Show them that you appreciate their efforts.

- Find out if you can help them.[4]

---

3   Cutting and sticking is *never* an excuse for your floor to look like a confetti factory. That's it. Teach the children to be bothered. Make it the case that they cut over the desk, put all leftover paper into the bin and pick up anything that's on the floor. I take pride in the fact that my cleaner (Sancha, since you ask) tells me how easy my room is to clean. On the rare day that there is mess, I always apologise and it's never seen as a problem.

4   A simple example here: do they want the chairs on the tables or left on the floor? I learned this at a school where I happened to be in my room and saw my cleaner (Phyllis – different school) taking all of the chairs down to clean the tables before putting them back up again. Realising that I'd added to her workload, I apologised and said I hadn't known this caused an issue. The school rule was for the children to put their chairs up at the end of the last lesson. From that simple interaction, Phyllis' life became easier *and* the school changed the rule.

Now to look at the other main groups of adults you work with.

OTHER TEACHERS, ESPECIALLY YOUR YEAR GROUP PARTNER

The size of your school, year group, management structure, day-to-day logistics and, of course, how sociable you are by nature will all determine how you go about interacting with other teaching staff, but here is some general guidance that has stood me in good stead for working with my year group partner and other close colleagues.

WORKING SMARTER TIPS

FIRST PLAN TOGETHER, THEN PLAN SEPARATELY

I addressed this in Chapter 2, but it's important enough to reiterate. Ensuring you collectively plan an overview of the topic so there is consistency between your classes is important, but then plan *specifically* for *your* class. After all:

● *You* know their needs best.

● *You* know what support they need.

● *You* know your teaching style.

Therefore, only you can plan effectively for your class.

MAKE SURE YOU SHARE RESOURCES

Ideally, you'll have a centralised area for this – we use Google Drive – but don't keep things you find or create to yourself. Here is a simple but effective guide:

1 Create/find.

2 Upload/share.

3 Inform partner of the presence of the new resource and how you plan to use it.

4 Move on.

Why step 4? Well, if you take the time to share a new resource which your partner then doesn't use, it can sting a bit, but don't take it personally. Maybe it wasn't ideal for their class (as we've just discussed). And, of course, the reverse can be true too, with you ignoring their precious resource. Share genuinely and openly without the pressure of trying to prove how wonderful you are and how grateful they should be for your input.

MAKE TIME TO SHARE STRATEGIES

This obviously relates to our previous points, but is more about *how* you teach. This, in my opinion, is one of the key elements of PPA that's often missed. It's even better if it can be paired with the opportunity to observe each other teach too.

It is fundamental that you approach this with an open mind and a genuine willingness to learn – regardless of your level of experience in the classroom. It is vital that, if you are more experienced or working with a new teacher, for example, you do not presume to be the expert on all things teaching. Be prepared to learn as much from them as they do from you, especially if you take the time to not only share, but to discuss and engage with ideas and concepts.

It was in this manner that I recently helped a new teacher add Dorothy Heathcote's Mantle of the Expert strategies to her classroom in ways she had not encountered before, while I was able to really up my game when it came to carpet time. We achieved this through discussion, questioning, observations and professional curiosity, humility and openness.

BE PREPARED TO DISCUSS YOUR CLASSES HONESTLY

Your year group partner will be having similar experiences and challenges, so ensure you make time to talk to each other about your classes and share ideas regarding how to resolve issues. I think it is especially important to take time to reflect on ideas that didn't quite work. Unfortunately, too often, a new idea can be rejected with little more than a 'Well, that was a waste of time, I won't be doing that again.' But if you're sharing strategies, and comfortable with observing each other, such 'failures' will offer opportunities to discuss, reflect and analyse and then plan for a new iteration. I've often found that it's during these discussions that I get my penny-drop moment, but the key here is being honest. I once worked with a colleague who, on the surface, appeared to have no problems. However, the class' performance, books and a few lesson observations painted a different story. It was only with the truth that we could move on. Therefore, it's important that you make time for each other and really build the relationship. Your year group partner will be your closest ally and support for the year, perhaps longer, so make time for each other – no excuses.

MAKE TIME TO CARE FOR EACH OTHER TOO

You'll have picked up a theme in the book so far and it is about building strong relationships. It's the same here. Make sure you take the time to find out about your year group partner's interests, partner's name (if they have one), children's names (if they have them) and other such personal details. The more you get to know them, the better you will be able to spot when they're tired/down/frustrated/overwhelmed/etc. And hopefully they can be there for you when you need it too.

Building that relationship will also help them feel comfortable confiding in you and allow you to confide in them too. For example, I once worked with a more experienced colleague who dreaded parents' evenings. Outwardly, she was loved by all and the model professional, but she had once had a bad experience and it still haunted her some 15 years after the event! Worse still, before me, she had never told anyone else. We worked together for two years and, once she told me, I helped make things easier by listening to her rehearse what she was going to say about each child. I would also be there on the night with a reassuring smile and, once I had learned that the reason why she never usually moved from her chair was so as not to draw attention to herself, to keep her topped up with tea and water.

It's easy to be solitary at work, cocooned in your own classroom, but making time for your year group partner and other close colleagues is vital – for both of you.

DON'T DELIBERATELY EXCLUDE ANYONE

You know how it makes you cross when a group of children deliberately exclude another from their play or work groups? You remember that episode of *Friends* when Rachel takes up smoking so as to not feel left out of the group of smokers her boss is in? Ever worked for a company where the important decisions are taken on the golf course and you hate golf? Well, don't treat your colleagues like that. Everyone deserves to be involved, with the opportunity to build trust, camaraderie and morale, and no one deserves to feel left out, especially when ideas are being discussed and decisions taken.

VARIETY IS THE SPICE OF LIFE

While I think that the relationship and bonds you forge with your year team are important, make sure that you branch out too. I learned this while working in a secondary setting when, inevitably, everyone tended to sit in their department groups. As much as I enjoyed being among the PE teachers sitting at the back, wearing shorts, eating cakes and having a laugh (if you've ever delivered a secondary INSET, you'll know who we were), it was only when we were made to sit in different groups that I realised the professional richness I was missing out on.

Ensure that you're mixing things up for your own professional benefit. Don't always sit with the same people or in the same space, whether that's at a staff briefing, an INSET day, a twilight CPD session or even during a coffee break.

TRIANGLES ARE STRONG STRUCTURES

One great way to ensure that we all work in a collaborative and supportive way beyond our year teams is to form triads. Colleagues are placed in a cross-phase group of three to work on ideas for whole-school or their own personal development. I have found that this approach is most successful when:

- The triads are given time to discuss teaching and learning.

- Everyone acknowledges what they are good at and/or enjoy doing.

- Each colleague decides on something that they want to try (hopefully something that is a strength of someone else in the triad).

- The triad plans together so they know the aims and purposes of one another's lessons.

- Two colleagues observe the other.

- There is a joint reflection session. This is very important. Plan to ensure that time considerations do not get in the way.

Working in this way is so much more productive and rewarding than a straightforward lesson observation is. Everyone knows what they are looking for and that what is being observed is not the teacher but the teaching, and especially the ideas you co-created. When done right, colleagues will be prepared to take risks as they know they can discuss what happened afterwards and reflect on their success – or otherwise.

For example, I was in one triad with a colleague who was keen to use music as part of her classroom management repertoire but did not have the knowledge or confidence to do so. She would certainly not have attempted it in a traditional lesson observation, feeling it to be too much of a high-risk strategy. However, the triad allowed us to discuss and plan together, especially as the other colleague and I both already used music in our lessons (we had read Nina Jackson's book[5] all about this), as audio cues, prompts, stimuli and for learning support. It then became part of this colleague's repertoire.

LSAs

I know that not every teacher will have an LSA – especially with budgets being squeezed more than ever. I have taught without an LSA on many occasions and while flying solo is a great confidence-builder, a great LSA is worth their weight in gold (yes, Sati, Louise, Caroline, Helen and Vikki – I mean all of you). Again, relationships are critical here. After all, you will be spending more time with them

---

5 N. Jackson, *The Little Book of Music in the Classroom: Using Music to Improve Memory, Motivation, Learning and Creativity* (Carmarthen: Crown House Publishing, 2009).

than you do with your partner and, unlike your partner, you may well have little say in who you end up with. Just think of Mr Poppy in *Nativity!*

Given the important role of the LSA in any class, it would be great to know that there had been some thought put into matching the LSA with the teacher, but I know that this is not always possible. Care really should be taken in matching the LSA to the class, however. Regardless of how you end up in this new special relationship, consider the following questions ...

AM I TAPPING INTO THEIR FULL POTENTIAL?

Frequently, like the office staff, LSAs will have a wealth of knowledge about the school, families and the community. They might be a parent of children at the school themselves. Don't let that insight go to waste.

Have they always been an LSA? What previous career experience, interests and hobbies do they have that could benefit your teaching or excite the children's learning? In the past I've had the pleasure of working with, to name but two, a geography graduate and a master potter, both of whom led sessions in their respective fields and gave the children a far better insight than I ever could. I also received some free CPD that I still use to this day. Imagine if all the teaching staff knew the strengths of your LSA and were able to draw on them as and when needed.

DO I SUPPORT THEM IN SUPPORTING ME?

As I mentioned in Chapter 2, lesson plans should be shown to your LSA. It's amazing how many colleagues – both teachers and LSAs – do not make this happen. I know time is a key factor in the success of this. However, I suggest the following approach:

START WITH AN ACCORD

Explain to your LSA how you plan lessons – as I've said before, I tend to use simple overview plans for the week with key information and children highlighted, with more detailed plans behind this. From there, agree how your LSA would like to receive the plans and what detail they want. For example, do they just want to know about their focus for the lesson and any children they'll be working with one-to-one, or would they rather know about everyone? In my experience, they will invariably want to know about everyone as they will want to see the big picture, which is what I want from them too.

MAINTAIN A PROFESSIONAL DIALOGUE

Once the planning is agreed, stick to it, but keep discussing it. Honest professional dialogue is vital for any healthy teacher–LSA relationship.

As we all know, the best LSAs will be reactive and responsive and use their knowledge, experience *and* intuition. In this way they will recognise when a child needs more, or less, support and intervention and can be prepared to go off-piste whenever necessary. Just make sure that this is not disruptive or in any way dismissive of your lesson (it can happen!). Remember, *you* are the teacher and responsible for the class' learning. But *always* discuss the learning, bearing in mind what the LSA could bring to the table.

START AS YOU MEAN TO GO ON

This is an extension to the advice I gave about transition, but once you know which class you will have and who your LSA will be, start talking to them. While they will still have a class to work with (although the LSA will often travel with the same class up through the school), as will you, a great way to start is to let them know the themes and topics you will be teaching next year. This has many benefits:

- It shows that you're including them immediately and starts to cement your relationship.

- They may have been involved in delivering the content before and can make suggestions.

- They may know where to find resources for the topic.

- They may be able to look out for resources or collect materials.

- It may be an area of interest for them or something they are an expert in.

- They could know great places to visit (especially if they are local to the school and you are not).

Related to this, make sure you inform your LSA what you're planning to deliver on transition day. While you may not have planned in as much detail as when you are teaching normally, this is also a great way to start the conversation and show them that you are bothered about including them and recognise the vital role they play.

AGREE A TIME AND STICK TO IT

Sharing your plans should always be done in a timely manner. Unless it's completely unavoidable, *don't* do this on a Monday morning. Enlightened schools will allocate some PPA at a designated time each week, so there is consistency, with more time that can be allocated depending on demands that arise in a particular week. My advice would be to give your LSA the plans for the following week straight after your PPA – this is when I provide mine with my lesson overviews at least.

Too often, LSAs either receive the planning late – just before the lesson or at the start of the day – or not at all. How can they support the children in that case? For anyone starting to form excuses in their head, I just ask, what if your own child was in that class and needed support? The LSA should be as prepared for the day as you are. Knowing what resources they will need, plus having some ready just in case, is something that can only be achieved if they receive the planning in a timely manner.

ASK FOR AND *ACCEPT* FEEDBACK

Unlike any observers from the SLT or Ofsted, your LSA will be in your room consistently and will see how you teach and the effect it's having over time. Indeed, when your plans don't work, they'll sometimes have to deal with the consequences. Be prepared to discuss with them how the lessons have gone and why some children did well while others seemed distracted or disaffected. Their view of your lesson is so much closer to the children's than yours and, as such, is invaluable.

The balance here is hard to strike, but if you've followed my previous points, hopefully this will be easier. You don't want sycophancy (however nice it may make you feel at the time) nor castigation and damnation (some LSAs are frustrated teachers), so get the balance right. I'd suggest recognising where a lesson 'went wrong' and using that as a point of discussion.

As an added bonus, if you are open to suggestions about how to improve your practice, news will get out and you won't be considered a potential know-it-all (a criticism often levelled at teachers by the wider school community, and deservedly so, in my experience), but instead someone who is human, humble and open to personal development.

ARE MY EXPECTATIONS CLEAR?

This is a tricky one, especially for less experienced teachers. Unfortunately, as with all adults, LSAs can be – ahem – elastic with their timings. An 8.30 am start means hitting the ground running at 8.30 am, not arriving then and making a coffee before getting down to work.

If this describes your LSA, rip off that particular plaster quickly, decisively and early. I've seen plenty of colleagues, including some who were very experienced, running around madly in the morning doing the job of two people rather than having 'that conversation' and reinforcing their – and the school's – expectations. You can save some early morning stress, as I advised in Chapter 1, by making sure your room is prepared the night before, but there's always more to cut out/laminate/mark/display/etc. Far better that your LSA is there with you, and you are getting jobs done together, spending time as a team and building your relationship.

MSAs

In many schools, thanks again to budgetary pressures, MSAs are all too frequently also LSAs, whether they offer general class support or work one-to-one with a specific child. This means their engagement with the children is maximised, but time for themselves is minimised, which, in itself, can create pressure to juggle their roles, the varying expectations the school has of them and the needs of their own bladder.

As I said in Chapter 3, there are ways to help your MSAs out, including being on duty every so often – even if you're not expected to be – and making sure you get out onto the playground *before* the end of lunch. However, here are a couple of MSA-specific working smarter tips.

WORKING SMARTER TIPS

REMEMBER THAT KNOWLEDGE IS POWER

Be prepared to speak to a couple of the MSAs before lunch starts if you have noticed that a child in your class has had a problem in the morning, especially if you've been keeping an eye on them at the request of a parent. This is far better than responding 'Oh yes, I know ...' when they speak to you at the end of lunch. This is dismissive. Perhaps, if they'd known, they could have kept an eye on, or been helpful in supporting, the child.

Similarly, when you go out at the end of lunch (a few minutes early, remember) make a point of approaching the MSAs to check how your class has been. Knowing of any issues or upsets ahead of time will smooth your afternoon and, by approaching them, you show that you want their input and that you value them.

Beyond these practical points, bear in mind that, like the office staff and LSAs, MSAs will frequently come from the local community and will often be mums from the school.[6] Therefore, they will have a great knowledge of the children and be able to support them, and you, accordingly. I've learned plenty of inside info from MSAs over the years, including:

- 'Their mum/dad has lost their job.'

- 'Their mum is pregnant again.'

- 'Their older sibling has just moved out.'

- 'Mum/dad has just got a new job.'

- 'They fell out with mum/dad this morning.'

So, use this intel to your benefit. Of course, if you're taking time on the playground with them, this information is often more forthcoming.

EMPOWER, DON'T DISEMPOWER

Time pressures and wanting to 'get on with learning' can make it easy to inadvertently disempower MSAs, so bear in mind that forewarned is forearmed. However, it is important to be supportive and work with MSAs over any issues that arise. Phrases such as, 'We'll deal with this inside', 'Thanks, I'll take it from here', and 'Yes, yes, yes, I get it', not only dismiss the problem but the MSA along with it, demeaning them in front of the children into the bargain. As long as the MSA is following school procedures, they need you to back them up. Of course, there is the occasional one who will want to bring back hanging for a seemingly trivial

---

6 Sorry, again, I honestly can't remember ever working with a dad in this role.

offence, but I'd suggest that this is more due to the demands on them than anything else. This makes it all the more important to ensure that you support them and recognise the constraints of their job. Furthermore, I know some people will claim that supporting an MSA following an incident will impact on teaching time; however, this shows the importance of getting onto the playground early and of informing them of any issues you know about ahead of time.

RECOGNISE THEM AS PART OF THE TEAM

This seems easy and obvious, but because of their working hours too often they're simply known as 'So and so's mum'. Be bothered enough to take at least a passing interest in their lives, as you would with any colleague. Yes, they may stand together and chat when they're supposed to be circling the playground individually. Yes, they may sometimes mishandle, avoid, or not handle incidents in the way that you would. Yes, you may think you could or would do it better. They might feel the same way about you based on what they pick up on the grapevine. But remember:

● They are the ones outside when it's blowing a hooley and the children are rampant, while we're inside.

● They are the ones outside when it's wet and miserable, knowing that bringing the children inside will impact on us teachers.

● They are the ones inside during wet play, while we remain in the sanctuary of the staffroom.

- They are the ones whose peace-keeping skills – in the face of footballing, friendship and fighting incidents – are worthy of the United Nations.

- They are the ones who can spot children – the ones in your class – who aren't part of group play.

- They are the ones who can spot someone – that child from your class – who is unusually upset.

- They are the ones who can spot someone who is hungry – and often find something for them to eat.

All these things make them vital to the school and, let's be honest, it's not as if they do it for the astronomical wages.

SLT

It has been said that one of the most important skills you can develop is learning how to manage those *above* you in an organisation. With that in mind, I want to share some thoughts about how to get the best out of your SLT.

Although the following is written as advice for class teachers regarding their working relationship with their school's leaders, I would recommend that it is read by leaders too.[7] It will help any SLT members to reflect on how to get the best out of their team – and what might be getting in the way of that. Certainly, writing this has caused me to reflect on several points in my practice.

---

7 Photocopy this section and slip it under the head's door in the dead of night if you need to!

First, it's only right to recognise that the term 'SLT' can mean a multitude of things, depending on your school. From one single head teacher to a whole team, from leaders who teach to those who don't, from those with vast experience across a number of schools to those with little, the landscape of our education system is remarkably diverse and this is reflected in those who lead it. Therefore, when looking at how *you* get the best out of your SLT, you will need to consider the structure of your school.

For example, a small (typically rural) school that has combined classes, few staff and a head teacher without any other senior managers is more likely – of necessity – to have a collegiate approach to decision making. By contrast, a larger primary, with a team of senior leaders and subject leaders, invariably has clear lines of command when it comes to decision making and processes.

What follows are some working smarter pointers that I have picked up over the years that I feel will help, regardless of where you work.

WORKING SMARTER TIPS

KNOW WHAT YOU WANT FROM LEADERS

Admittedly, this may be trickier for an early career teacher (ECT), but before joining a school, be honest about what you want – and need – as a professional. I've spoken previously about the recruitment and retention crisis in education, and this can work to your advantage. Be prepared to be choosy and look beyond the school website or information pack – glossy or otherwise – that you are sent. Before applying, ask yourself five simple questions:

1 Where am I in my career?

2 What do I need in order to make progress?

3 What ambition do I have?

4 What areas do I need to develop?

5 What do I bring to the table?

The important thing here is to answer these questions honestly – not just because they're likely to come up in an application or interview, but because if you know this about yourself then you can research the school you're applying to properly and with purpose.

After you've applied – presuming that you've seen nothing to put you off as a result of your answers to the five questions – prepare yourself for how you would answer these questions in an interview. Leaders are far more likely to want to explore your aspirations if raised at this point than if they are hit with a list of demands and expectations after you start.

Incidentally, don't underestimate the importance of question 5. Recognise your strengths – both from your previous teaching experience and from beyond the classroom – and find out how they could be exploited in your new role, but in a mutually acceptable manner. If your interview admission of 'I like to play the piano' is understood as meaning 'I want to be involved in every assembly sing-song, the Christmas carol concert and the end-of-year show', you may wish you had kept it quiet!

KNOW WHO DOES WHAT

This is a ridiculously simple piece of advice, but I've always been amazed that some staff members don't know everyone on their SLT and what they all do.[8] Part of this is knowing the hierarchy – real and perceived – within the SLT. While the assistant head may be the person who is always seen around the school, the deputy head is actually the second in command and may not take too kindly if this is not recognised. Also, knowing the hierarchy means you will know who to go to when you need help, whether it's regarding a new initiative, some support you require or a good idea you've had.

While parents may think that they can go straight to the head – and it can be frustrating when they are allowed to and teachers are cut out of the process, I know – you should really respect the established order of things. When you do, it can save you time and effort and it also ensures that the lines of communication flow smoothly. Which brings me to ...

KNOW HOW THEY COMMUNICATE (AND WHAT THEY MEAN)

Although most schools will communicate largely via email these days, working out whether someone prefers a face-to-face chat is invaluable. I for one much prefer some proper facetime, especially as I can pick up the nuances that are potentially lost in an email. It also means bypassing those long, often irrelevant,

---

8 Of course, my assumption here is that they do all, in fact, do something.

email threads. And don't get me started on 'reply all' follow-up conversations! That said, following up a personal conversation with an email along the lines of 'Thanks for your time earlier, I appreciated talking about ...' is always good form and does provide evidence if you need a paper trail of what was discussed and when.

I also sincerely recommend learning to spot the difference between staff opinions genuinely being sought and paying lip service to a decision that has already been taken. This way, you won't spend unnecessary hours thinking through and outlining your thoughts by way of a response that will only fall on deaf ears. Of course, if opinions are really being sought, take the time to share yours – whether it is voicing agreement or raising a question or two. Show that you are bothered and that you are prepared to use your voice. That way, no one can accuse you of not speaking up when given the opportunity and it also means you won't waste unnecessary energy grumbling after the event.

ASK THE SLT WHAT, WHY AND HOW

One of the biggest problems I see in schools is the lack of clarity. Believe me, while it might not seem like it, leaders don't go out of their way to obfuscate and confuse. However, what might be clear in the head's head might not look that way by the time it gets to yours. Opting for a position of 'knowledge is power' will help you much more than one of 'ignorance is bliss'. So, if you are unclear, ask. Always. And if that still doesn't satisfy that uneasy feeling in your stomach, ask why.

Do this not to be a member of the awkward squad but because it will help you do the job you are being asked to do better.

Finally, and importantly for stressed and burnt-out teachers, be prepared to ask how. If your SLT launches new initiatives in the same way that they let off party poppers at a staff do, it's not unreasonable to ask how you're going to fit this latest big thing in alongside the initiative they launched last week and the one from the week before that. I've lost count of the things I have seen come and go – some never to come back again – and there's a lot to be said for (metaphorically) standing still.

That said, think about the lines of communication and how this genuine concern can best be raised. Maybe through a one-to-one chat or at a team meeting, during which the initiative or policy can be discussed in greater detail. Maybe it really isn't as bad as you think? Also, especially in a key stage meeting, members of the SLT will be present and, hopefully, will listen and feed back concerns that are genuinely and professionally put.

MEET DEADLINES

This isn't a piece of advice for working with the SLT per se, but when you are asked to do something by a specific time, make sure you do so – properly and correctly – even if you don't agree with it. Missing deadlines causes a backlog which will have knock-on consequences for you, your colleagues and potentially the children too. Hopefully, the timelines have been considered (ideally, working backwards from the end point[9]) so deadlines are reasonable, as much as is possible in a busy school.

SEEK ADVICE

The leaders of the school have a responsibility for and a duty towards your development and progress, so make sure that you ask for the help and support you need. They may always seem busy, especially if they have their own class to teach too, but you must make contact – and do so sooner rather than later. If you have a member of the SLT in your key stage, they will be your first port of call, although ensuring you know who does what means you can also go direct to the source for support. Always be prepared to ask, especially if it involves the progress and success of a child in your class, even more so if it is about well-being or safeguarding.

This point also applies to your own personal development. If you aspire to leadership, in any form beyond your current position, speak to the SLT (remember, they have been there too) and gain their insights. They will probably be able to cover most areas of aspiration and, if not, will certainly be able to direct you to the correct points of contact.

---

9 A great example of this is the annual (or termly, depending on your school) report. Working back from the day they will be distributed, there should be a timeline for data input, writing, checking, editing, printing, signing, collating and putting in envelopes. Yet I have only worked in one school where every deadline was kept by everyone. You not writing them in time – for whatever reason, and I think I've heard them all – means that leaders lose time to check them and so on. I once worked in a school that ended up shutting the office for an entire day to get the reports out on time due to slippage further up the timeline.

FOR BETTER AS WELL AS FOR WORSE

I have known colleagues who will turn to the SLT only when they are at the end of their tether or they want something, or someone, 'dealt with'.[10] But why do they not show them the positives too? Play your part by ensuring that excellent – truly excellent – work is seen by your SLT. You can do this by:

- Directing them when they visit the class.

- Sending children to them with work.

- Making sure you have a clearly visible WAGOLL (what a good one looks like) wall.

- Sharing successes with parents (who will feed it back to the SLT in turn).

- Using the school's social media platforms for communication. Any SLT worth their salt will be tapped into that.

- Making the most of those incidental opportunities to share good news – when they're on the playground, at the gate or in the staffroom, for example.

One final word of advice here. Ensure that the focus of these interactions is your learners and not you. For example:

---

10 Admittedly, some leaders bring this perception upon themselves, rarely being seen outside of their office apart from to 'deal with things' or introduce the INSET speaker before sweeping out of the hall to get on with 'more important' matters.

'Jessica, show Miss Begum that amazing story opener you constructed independently.'

'Ali, get your sketchbook out to show Mr Angelos the way you added detail to your work the other day.'

These are both great ways to show and share a child's success, unlike:

'Aisha, tell Ms Reddy what we've been doing in history.'

'Aadesh, explain to Mrs Davies what you learned about reading a line graph.'

The none-too-subtle subtext of these directions is 'Hey, children, tell the head what a great teacher I am' – something a teacher may do to show off or out of insecurity and the need for reassurance and validation.

REMEMBER THAT THE SLT ARE PEOPLE TOO

Like all of us, school leaders need appreciation and praise too. Being a leader isn't easy and is often – usually – thankless.[11] How often do you take the time to say thank you or well done to them, and genuinely mean it? It is the work of but a moment yet could make their day. For example, if you particularly liked their assembly, say so. If their training, or part of it, engaged you, made you think, stirred you to action or just kept you

---

11 How many were personally thanked for shouldering the stresses and strains of running their school through the COVID-19 pandemic, for example?

awake, tell them. If they do something supportive – speak with a child, help you with a parent, model a lesson, engage in a chat at breaktime, cover for you, or even cancel a meeting that can be covered in an email instead – thank them.

It is through such little acts that entire cultures can be changed.

CHAPTER CONTEMPLATIONS

In writing this chapter, I really wanted to get you to think about your relationships with colleagues and to recognise the importance of each individual, not only to you, but to the whole school. It's all too easy in the time-pressured situations we find ourselves in each day to become like tortoises, retreating into our own shells, just barely poking our heads out in order to grab a coffee or get some last-minute photocopying done.

Remember, the aim of this book is to make your life easier and to allow you to be the best version of your teaching self that you can be. All of the adults discussed in this chapter will help you achieve that, if you let them. Recognise, too, that there will be others – one-to-one support staff, kitchen staff, therapy staff, intervention teachers, reading recovery colleagues and more. The tips in this chapter will help you work with them all, so please do stop and reflect on how you currently work with them.

When considering your approach to working with adults, ask yourself ...

● Am I making the best possible use of that colleague?

- Do I know how that colleague can improve my teaching – and hence my class' learning?

- Do I make time for the adults I work with?

- Do I show my colleagues that I am bothered about them through my day-to-day interactions?

- Am I inclusive?

- Do I actively seek out opportunities to learn from others?

And, for me, the key to my teaching, as set in motion over 25 years ago by my friend and mentor Daryll Chapman:

- Do I see the person behind the non-teaching role?

CHAPTER 7

A MISCELLANY OF SMART WAYS OF WORKING

Throughout this book I have tried to identify smart ways of working that will empower you by freeing up time and energy. Apart from wanting to make life less stressful for you, I have also made sure that the content is all, genuinely, based on lived classroom experience.

Being smart about how you work can be seen as lazy by those who seem to prefer the hamster wheel approach to the day job,[1] but I hope you've seen that it doesn't *have* to be this way in primary teaching. You really can be smarter, do things differently and get the same – if not better – results.

In this final chapter I will deal with smarter ways of working across topics that didn't seem to fit naturally into any other chapter. It's a miscellany but an important one all the same, and I'm starting with a weekly occurrence in many schools.

---

1   And do check out Jim Smith's *The Lazy Teacher's Handbook* if you are inspired by the idea of getting the class to work harder than you do! J. Smith, *The Lazy Teacher's Handbook: How Your Students Learn More When You Teach Less*, new edn (Carmarthen: Independent Thinking Press, 2017).

STAFF MEETINGS

Meetings are a necessary part and parcel of life in all schools and come in many shapes and sizes – those for phase or key stage, weekly training, whole-staff, classroom-based staff, not to mention ECT, subject leader, SLT and more. I'll share some working smarter tips that work for them all, whether you're leading the meeting or on the receiving end of it.

Let's start by being honest. How often have you come out of a meeting thinking, 'Well that's an hour of my life I'll never get back'? Then think about how creative we became during the 2020–2021 lockdowns with the way we handled meetings, either virtually or socially distanced. We did away with many of them completely. As life gets back to normal, we have a chance to be a lot smarter about meetings – how we conduct them and, importantly, whether we need them in the first place. So what follows are some questions for your consideration.

DO WE REALLY NEED THAT MEETING?

Now we're talking! Or, rather, maybe talking isn't what's needed and we could manage to achieve the same – or better – results with an email, a Doodle poll, a Google Form, a team WhatsApp chat or any other quick and easy, technology-based way of getting a message across. Let all the hassle and heartache of keeping a school running through an extended period of lockdown not be in vain.

Notwithstanding this, we must also recognise that often the most important element of a meeting isn't what is discussed but the fact that everyone is together (and can have conversations either side of the 'important stuff'). With that in mind, think about how the meeting time will best be used. The meeting just before the end of term when colleagues are jaded and need a boost is important. As is the one following a particularly tough week. If you've sensed that a meeting is needed – or, rather, a coming together of the troops under the pretence of a meeting – then consider the content carefully:

- How can you make it fun and uplifting, or at least add fun elements to it?

- Could one of the SLT or subject leaders model a learning practice they have delivered or witnessed and engage the staff with some collaborative learning, while providing some together time?

- Alternatively, could you hold discussion forums on teaching and learning, which will allow you to come together as professionals?

- Is there a direction of travel you wish to discuss – for example, some exciting future plans for the school?

- Have the staff identified any training needs? Could you create groups to address this in a positive, not deficit-driven, manner?

One of my best examples of this was when my school recognised the need for greater coherence over our expectations regarding clay work in art. One meeting consisted of having everyone work in their year teams to create pieces they would expect from their children, before annotating the skills they would want to teach and demonstrate. By doing this together, and practically, colleagues could discuss what would be different between Years 1 and 2, and 2 and 3, so we established a clear sense of progression.

This was done in July, with clay for everyone to use (cue giggles from staff of a certain age as they recreated the pottery scene from *Ghost*), and the succeeding year's clay work was better planned, better linked to other curriculum areas (invariably, though not exclusively, history), and *everyone* had a laugh together, leaving with a smile on their faces and feeling that they had achieved something tangible and useful.

WHO IS THE MEETING FOR?

Does everyone in attendance actually need to be there? Do they need to be there for the whole meeting? Could they attend for the start and then return to their own areas to work? Would breaking into smaller groups (who can reconvene and feed back if necessary) be better, for example?

For some reason, regardless of the school, the EYFS team seem to bear the brunt of the 'all must attend' approach. They are clearly more patient and tolerant than I am, as I have lost count of the number of times I have heard comments like 'I'm not sure how this will work for you' or 'This next bit doesn't really apply to you.' Yet they still sit there smiling, when there's clearly a multitude of better things they could be doing.

Simply put, if someone, anyone, doesn't need to be there, don't make them. Treat them like professionals and let them choose how to better use their time.

WHAT'S THE NUMBER ONE MESSAGE YOU WANT STAFF TO TAKE AWAY FROM THE MEETING?

Nobody will remember everything that's covered in a meeting, so concentrate on what you want colleagues to take away and keep it clear and simple. I find that the old adage about public speaking works well here:

- Say what you're going to say – preferably before the meeting, as well as at the start.

- Say it – which will also involve staff engagement in some form.

- Say what you've said – in a few simple concise sentences to ensure everyone has understood the same message.

This means everyone knows what they're coming to, can be prepared, and leaves knowing what will happen next.

DO YOU TREAT THE MEETING WITH IMPORTANCE?

You've decided to get everyone together, you've blown the biscuit budget and you've prepared the room (considering the seating, lighting and heating). The stage is set but if the management of the meeting is poor, you are sending a clear but unintended message. If you want the meeting treated with the importance you feel it should have, by all concerned, then consider the following:

- Set an agenda – no one should arrive at the meeting not knowing what it's about (but too many do).

● Provide minutes[2] – too many schools leave colleagues to make their own notes and come to their own interpretation. A set of minutes sent out within 24 hours (48 at most) will ensure the message, follow-up actions and expectations are clear for everyone. Also ensure that the minutes are available on the school's shared area, however this is organised.[3]

● Provide any relevant documents that will be referred to *before* the meeting so that colleagues can prepare – expect them to have read the material and be ready for the meeting. In doing so, you are treating them as the professionals they are.

● Start on time – having a clearly defined start, and sticking to it, is important and gives the clear message that the meeting is important too. Agree on the best start time – one that realistically caters for colleagues who may need to speak to parents, deal with uncollected children, get a coffee, have a toilet break and the likes first – and stick to it.

Your role in leading a meeting, or even leading part of it, calls upon you to know your script and to deliver it clearly and confidently.[4] All too often, these two fundamentals are forgotten. I know that, as teachers, we present to others almost every minute of every working day, but we need to appreciate that presenting to colleagues is a different kettle of fish.

By taking the time to plan and prepare fully, you are giving the meeting – and your colleagues' time – the respect it

---

2   I would suggest asking one of the office staff to take these, type them up and send them out. Allowing an early departure another day as time off in lieu is an idea that keeps everyone happy, I have found.

3   See Appendix 3 for a suggestion of how to create simple, focused action minutes.

4   If you're nervous, it is OK to rehearse. Work with a trusted colleague on this, especially if you have seen them successfully lead a meeting.

deserves, and that will pay dividends. Remember too, your colleagues will be tremendously forgiving, especially as many will be thinking 'Thank God it's not me leading this meeting!'

WORKING SMARTER TIPS

ASK YOURSELF WHAT YOUR PRESENTATION SAYS ABOUT YOU

If the meeting involves you giving a presentation, the advice you give to the children in your class applies to you too – you are the main event, not the PowerPoint, no matter how many whacky fonts you use, animations you employ or funny memes you've found on Facebook that you add in. You present, and the slides – or any other form of aid or prop – are there to support and enhance what you say. Again, seek out people who come across well when presenting and think about how they do that.

Some other tips, drawn from years of experience of sitting in awful meetings, include:

- Do a run-through. I would recommend that all presentations are shared with the SLT before being delivered to the whole school. If you're too nervous to seek out and accept feedback, then you are too dangerous to be unleashed on the whole staff with a projector.

- Know the room. Be prepared to project your voice to the back of the hall if necessary.

- Check that your slides can be seen from *anywhere* in the room. If using text, make sure it's legible for everyone. I've lost count of how many times I've been asked if I can read the text from the back of the room and then been told it doesn't matter when I can't.

- Make sure that your slides have more pictures than text (less is definitely more when it comes to text in PowerPoint), a grown-up typeface (Helvetica is ideal, though Arial Black works well too) and a decent-sized font (36 is my lucky number).

- Make it a story. We know from how we frame the curriculum (see Chapter 2 for a reminder) that this is how learners work best, so craft the story of your presentation to genuinely engage.

- Use humour. Even a poor joke usually gets a smile because it is better than being boring. Use that meme you found on Facebook if necessary.

- It's the audience's job to read the slides, not yours.

- I repeat, it's the audience's job to read the slides, not yours. If there is some important information that you need to read, such as specific facts and figures to prove a point, make sure you have the slides on presenter view so you can use the notes function. Standing in one place for this part of the presentation helps. This means that there is limited or no text for colleagues to read, so instead they listen to you.[5]

---

5   Cognitive load theory applies here and this is a useful article to help you if you're new to it, or have heard the term but want to understand more how it can affect you and your learners: D. Shibli and R. West, Cognitive Load Theory and Its Application in the Classroom, *Impact: Journal of the Chartered College of Teaching* (February 2018). Available at: https://impact.chartered.college/article/shibli-cognitive-load-theory-classroom/.

● If there's an important message to take away or action to follow up on, provide a briefing sheet which goes beyond what will be in the minutes. This could be further reading or a pro forma. If you are including an exemplar, cover more than just the year group you teach.

● There is rarely any need to have the entire presentation sent out or printed off for everyone either, especially if, as I recently experienced, the printed slides are just a miniature version of what was too small to read on the screen. If there is a need for colleagues to have all or some of the presentation, put it on the shared area to save time, money, effort, ink and trees.

DISPLAY BOARDS

Before offering any tips here, I have to ask, what's your school policy? This is an even more important question if you are reading this as the policy maker – especially as, in my experience, those making the decisions about displays are either not in the classroom full time (and might have forgotten the time pressures on busy class teachers) or are display fanatics with a zeal for decorative boards generated by some burning/failed/frustrated ambition to be an artist. It's a display board, not the Selfridges Christmas window!

As you can perhaps tell, I really don't get as excited about display boards as those who have found their 'display tribe' on Pinterest or Instagram. But they are a part of school life, which means we need to get back to basics when it comes to being smart about how we use them. Which means asking the million-dollar question: what is this display board for?

Recognising that display boards, depending on their location, serve different functions will help with the answer to this question because, as I see it, there are four distinct types. Once we know what sort of board we are dealing with, we can examine each in turn.

1. THE CENTRAL INFORMATION AND/ OR PROMOTIONAL BOARD

Is it in a central location, often by the school office or the main hall? If so, its purposes will include:

● Information or message sharing – the closer to the main office the truer this is. It can often include a digital display of some kind these days.

● Promotion of an activity – this is especially true around Christmas.

● Sensory and learning stimulation. This is a school after all.

● Creating a sense of unity around shared projects – for example, promoting reading or themed events, like the harvest festival or Easter.

2. THE CORRIDOR BOARD

These have different focuses and purposes, including:

● Learning stimulation – this should always be linked to actual learning, not just some esoteric downloaded pieces that look nice.

- Sensory stimulation – corridors are powerful influencers of mood and atmosphere and can help your learners learn.[6] This is also why the colours on the walls are important, so do your research and choose carefully.

- Challenging children to pause and wonder. I have seen whole corridors turned into cabinets of curiosity.[7]

- Stimulating engagement with a sneak preview of learning to come.

- Creating a sense of unity with shared projects – for example, reading displays or sharing whole-school projects and events such as Remembrance Day.

- Creating a sense of unity through sharing learning. For example, at my current school the history leader has curated a timeline that shows what each year group is learning in history, demonstrating how it fits within an overall chronology.

3. THE UNIFYING, COLLABORATIVE, COMMUNAL BOARD

If you have responsibility for any areas within school, it is likely that you may well have to create communal displays. So, in addition to the tips I've shared so far, here are a few more ways to make your life as easy as possible:

- Make sure – as much as you can, given your pay grade – that the school only uses decent boards, ideally

---

6   Visit your EYFS department to see what I mean!

7   Check out *The Little Book of Awe and Wonder* by Dr Matthew McFall's for more on this: M. McFall, *The Little Book of Awe and Wonder: A Cabinet of Curiosities* (Carmarthen: Independent Thinking Press, 2013).

framed and of good quality. Add some new ones each year if you can't afford them all at once.

- If you have decent boards, *never* back them. It's a waste and the paper always needs replacing.

- Never mount work. It's time-consuming and a faff (see my advice on work frames on page 208).

- Use pins, not staples. Whoever has the staple remover is ruler of the whole kingdom, but no one ever knows who it is. Why risk your nails or a knife when pins are easier to remove and allow the children to put displays up and take them down more easily?

- Remember that less is more. The board doesn't need to be completely full. Blank space draws the eye and shows off what is there. Think of art galleries.

- Rotate rather than change. Can the board be developed and allowed to evolve rather than changed completely every few weeks?

- Making changes once a term is fine. Recognise that displays are time-consuming, so one change per term is enough to keep the display fresh but the task manageable.

- Displaying photocopies of work is fine. Simply put, we don't always have time to get the class to craft a final, finished piece and if we do have the time, why aren't we using it for more fun learning? What's more, some children will never get their work on display as they will never finish a 'display-worthy' piece, or they'll put so much effort into redrafting it that writing it out again will be a chore. Using a photocopied version of a second draft is fine.

- Edits are fine. Don't let the children think that their work has to be error-free to be on display. This isn't realistic and also doesn't display the genuine process of learning. Celebrate and highlight edits and improvements.

- Treat it like a working wall. Too often, colleagues become slaves to display, and not through choice. Instead, it's far better to craft a display over time, something which builds anticipation for the children and allows you to manage your time more effectively, rather than having to get in by 7 am and staying after school until the site manager kicks you out.

- Create a 'watch this space' vibe. It helps build anticipation and curiosity, which is great for learning. Get some sacking/fabric/opaque plastic, cover the board, put a great big sign on it saying 'Under construction'. Even better, get some hazard tape. Craft your display over time, as suggested in the previous point. For added theatre, try to ensure that you are 'caught' replacing the sacking over the display and swear your co-conspirators to secrecy, before you're finally ready to reveal it.

When considering communal display boards, ask yourself ...

HOW DO I INVOLVE THE CHILDREN?

This can be forgotten when working on communal displays, but having the children involved will not only empower them, but also free you up. They can contribute ideas, research and pupil voice, as well as the work, and, if you can stand the abdication of power, they can put it up too.

HOW DO I INVOLVE OTHER STAFF?

If you make communal displays an opportunity to share the children's work, then you can get staff involved in helping you. Amazingly, if everyone contributes something, you will quickly fill a display – especially if you go for a 'less is more' philosophy.

HOW DO I SHOW IT OFF?

Use the school's social media profiles to share this with parents and let them know why it's important. If it's just to fill a space, and what you're sharing is along the lines of 'Look at our lovely display of downloaded images for harvest', then ask why you need the display in the first place. It's also important to show it off to the children, so do you take them to look at it? Do you pause to discuss a display and highlight any recent changes to it? Do you encourage your class to keep an eye on any unexpected changes?

HAVE YOU CONSIDERED WORK FRAMES?

Just as you celebrate work in the classroom, so should you celebrate it in corridors. Working to whatever budget you have, buying proper art frames – even better, ones with doors – to show off examples of excellence is a powerful statement. All the teacher needs to do is write a note explaining why a particular piece of work has been chosen. Or, better yet, ask a member of the SLT, or even a visitor, to choose a stand-out piece of work that they have spotted on a classroom visit or walkabout.

Again, this should be celebrated, shared and generally made a big fuss of, particularly through social media. A nice touch is to get a video of the child and the teacher explaining the work and why it was chosen, which can then be uploaded to the school website.

My only rule here is that it really must celebrate true excellence, not just be a way to boost self-esteem. ('Whose turn is it in the gilded frame of happiness this week, children?') Address self-esteem in whatever other ways you have at your disposal but save this display so it means something special to all those whose work ends up in it.

Another easy win here is to transfer the work onto a nearby board once it comes out of the frame – after three weeks or so seems about right. This board will grow and develop over the academic year and, if you are canny about the number of frames you use (it doesn't need to be one per class), it will only need to be taken down at the end of the year.

4. THE CLASSROOM BOARD

I have already mentioned the use of boards for classroom management in Chapter 1 and asked you to consider how you use displays for promoting times tables in Chapter 4. However, in my room display boards have other purposes:

- Working boards (for all subjects) – supporting what's being learned.[8]

- Recall boards – reminders of what has been learned.

- Activation boards – engaging learning with previews of what is to come.

- Reading boards – we use this to operate a book recommendation scheme.[9] Once a child has completed a book, they write a review and post their

---

8   The most important board, in my opinion, followed by the recall board.
9   This is my only real 'display' in the traditional sense, with prepared materials such as book covers on display.

recommendation in someone else's envelope, so we have a board of envelopes (one for each child), with a display full of age-appropriate books.

- Celebration boards – sharing the children's best work (e.g. a WAGOLL wall).

- Information boards – containing the seating plan, timetable, lunch menu, etc.

- Activity boards – challenges for the children to undertake should they finish the task set (to a high standard and meeting all criteria, of course).

Although these are my preferred ways of working with boards in my classroom, yours may differ based upon classroom size, the amount of wall space you have, school expectations and the likes. However, when considering classroom display boards, I would also suggest that you ask yourself ...

HOW CLEAR IS THE INTERACTIVE WHITEBOARD?

Sometimes, class teachers can get a bit too liberal with displays, especially with reminders located at the front of the room where the instructions/task/information is shared.

Whatever is on the interactive whiteboard, it needs to be free from distractions so that the children can focus on the learning and not the peripheral paraphernalia, which can lead to cognitive overload and overstimulation. This is important for all learners, not just those identified with SEND issues. Ideally, all display boards will be set away from the interactive whiteboard. But, as you probably had no hand in the design of your room, do your best to not allow displays to encroach.

DO YOU KNOW WHAT A WORKING WALL REALLY IS?

It can be easy to lose sight of the purpose of a working wall, especially if, as a leader, it's been a while since we have been fully engaged in the classroom. A working wall should *not* have glossy, printed pictures on it, for example. Instead, it is there to support the work, showing models for the children to follow and apply in their learning. To this end, flip charts are a great resource as they are ideal for modelling work. The used paper can be put up on the working wall, which saves you having to create a display from scratch. This approach has the added advantage of supporting the children with their recall, as they were present when the example was created: something you can draw on with sensitive, tactical questioning.

DO YOUR DISPLAYS EVOLVE?

Related to the previous point, try to think about how your modelling can be added to over time. You know what you will be teaching in future lessons, so your display can grow and build on the foundational knowledge you have already laid down. Not only does this make it easier to grow the display, but it keeps a familiar reference point for the children, so new models can build and expand on existing ones. Here's an example I have used recently in maths to highlight my point:

- When modelling how to record times tables, I used 7 x 9 = 63 (mainly because I had seen the children struggle with this in the Times Tables Rock Stars heat maps – see Chapter 3).

- We could then extend our learning by using 7 x 9 = 63 as a base fact, and see how 70 x 9 = 630, 0.7 x 9 = 6.3, etc.

- I developed this further when modelling language and multiplication/division calculations (e.g. factors, multiples, multiplier, multiplicand and product).

- This was then used to show how 63 is not a prime number as it has more than two factors, so it has to be a composite number.

- I then extended the model to show 63's prime factors, breaking down 7 x 9 to 7 x 3 x 3.

- Finally, when we moved on to measuring areas, I could use all of this not only to model how to calculate area, but also how to solve a missing side question, where the answer was 63cm².

This meant that the children had foundational knowledge to build on as we went through the learning, and I only needed to add to the board – not reinvent it – as we went along.

DO YOU HAVE A MIX OF BOARDS?

Magnetic whiteboards are ideal for working walls as the content can be more easily edited, annotated and changed. If you can, I would suggest having all whiteboards, as work can be displayed just as effectively as on a traditional board, but they can be used for a different purpose if you so desire. Having a mix of traditional boards and magnetic whiteboards is not a bad compromise.

HAVE YOU CONSIDERED THE LOCATIONS OF YOUR BOARDS?

First, how you designate your boards is important and needs careful consideration. As they will be used daily, the numeracy and literacy boards should be towards the front of the class, with other subject boards around the room.

Second, if you don't like how your boards are arranged, look at getting them moved. Follow my advice in Chapter 6 and you'll soon be besties with the site manager, who will be happy to help, especially if you explain why you are making the move. Ensure you've thought about it, though, as you don't want to have to ask again, and you might want to check it's OK to do so too with your key stage leader or a member of the SLT.[10]

It is also worth considering how you could best use the windows. You can get special pens for writing on glass – although normal whiteboard pens can be used too – and there's nothing wrong with putting flipchart paper up on the windows either, depending upon the glare of the sun and ensuring you are not cutting out that all-important natural light.

ARE YOU OVERCOMPLICATING YOUR CLASSROOM DISPLAYS?

As I said at the outset of this section, I don't get as excited or agonised about displays as many others do, and I have never, ever been into school during the holidays to create and curate displays for the children to be enthralled by (briefly) on the first day back. I prefer to keep things simple. Filling the space with PDF printouts is not a good use of anyone's time or money, so ensure that everything on display is there for a purpose. Purposeful, targeted working walls are far better than pre-created displays, especially when you empower the learners and give them responsibility for helping curate the boards.

Similarly, when labelling boards, do so by subject, not topic. What you're teaching should be obvious from what's on the board (for example, the label should read 'History', not 'The Greeks'). A simple idea for this is to use a

10 Or you could just go for it. It's your room, after all.

set of letter tiles to spell out the subject's name (get in touch and I can email a set to you). Better yet, handwrite the lettering so you can model the school's handwriting policy, or create your own computer version if, like me, your handwriting is not exactly policy standard.

MOVEMENT

I have touched on this previously – notably when talking about getting attention in Chapter 1 and playtime in Chapter 3 – but I wanted to bring together some ideas on the topic. Why? Because I have witnessed an inordinate amount of time being lost due to poor planning – or no planning – when it comes to movement, leading to what can best be described as 'a kerfuffle'.

Even though in a primary school there is less need for movement around the school than there is in a secondary school, it still needs to be considered properly, so ask yourself ...

DO I HAVE A CLEAR, CONSISTENT SIGNAL FOR THE CLASS?

As I said regarding assemblies in Chapter 1, ensure the children know the signal and make it clear and consistent. I prefer going with 'Show me you're ready for ...' as I have taught the children what I mean – stand up, chairs under tables, be quiet. This saves me repeating instructions or commands and works for whatever event we are preparing for. Plus, it affords me the opportunity to thank those who are ready and encourage others to catch up, rather than crossly singling out those who are still talking, turning around, faffing about and the likes.

DO I MOVE THE CLASS WITH A PURPOSE?

I admit that many children have commented (or com-plained) that I walk fast. It's the PE teacher in me. However, I don't see this as a bad thing, I just point out that we have important things to do and that I want to get on with doing them. I have occasionally been asked what it is that I'm in such a hurry to achieve and the reply is always the same: learning.

You may need to start early to get them into the habit of walking with purpose, especially those who have been used to dawdling, but by creating the sense of team we focused on earlier, the children will move with you and at your pace.

DO I TAKE TIME TO PAUSE EVERY SO OFTEN?

Whether it is pausing on your journey in from break to consider the clouds, the leaves, a bird, the smell in the air or the breeze on your face, or in the corridor to listen to singing coming from the hall or to look at a communal display board, I think W. H. Davies' words in his celebrated poem 'Leisure' should be a guide for all teachers, however busy they think their day is:

What is this life if, full of care,

We have no time to stand and stare?

W. H. DAVIES

HOW DO I BALANCE MOVEMENT AND ORGANISATION?

All too often, especially with boys, movement can descend into chaos while the line is being 'organised'. Not only is there too much fuss about who is first, who is pushing in and who's held whose place, there is also the opportunity for lollygagging. Therefore, sometimes you just need to set off. The children will fall into line accordingly. And don't even think about trying those pretend responsibility roles I mentioned in Chapter 1.

That said, there will be times when you do need to ensure organisation – for example, for school trips or at the start of term. Take the time to get the class organised. What follows are some pointers to help organise the children:

- Exit in table groups – an orderly movement, but with some freedom about who they walk in front of and behind.

- Alphabetical order – ideal for fire drills so there's no organisation needed on the playground and for photograph day so you're not herding cats in front of the photographer.

- In columns – if your classroom is organised as such. Those nearest the door exit first, avoiding the amazing primary school phenomenon of the boy furthest from the door exiting before the girl closest to it, something which usually has a lot to do with playing football.

Finally, ensure that your approach to movement is consistent and that the class know that being calm and quick is a non-negotiable expectation – one that relates to coming back from playtime as well as heading out.

PARENTS

This topic could be a whole book in itself! I have covered some elements of parental engagement in Chapter 1 when discussing routines and in Chapter 3 with unhomework. However, this is an area that colleagues who I've spoken to are frequently concerned about and feel is all too neglected. In a book all about working smarter, I feel that parents merit their own section as they play a huge role in primary education, particularly if you want them to engage with the many areas of schooling where their assistance is vital – from reading with their children, helping with home learning, and attending meetings and events to accompanying trips and visits and generally supporting your work in the classroom.

In the same way that everyone knows how to be the England football manager or prime minister, everyone knows how to be a teacher. Except they don't. At least this perception was sorely dented during lockdown, when parents around the world finally had more than an inkling about what the job of a primary teacher involves.[11]

What we in the profession need to bear in mind is that parents do want to support their children. I can honestly say, in all my years of teaching, I have never yet met a parent who *wanted* to fail their child or for their child to fail. The challenge is – as it has always been – those who are not best equipped to support them, or who do not embrace the school's ethos and approaches, even if they went to that school themselves as a child. Sometimes, *especially* if they went to that school as a child.

Remember, being a teacher requires training, qualifications, reflection and continual observation – you have to hold yourself up to the prescribed high standards, whereas being a parent simply requires you to have a child. We are the professionals here, so we need to be the ones leading when it comes to building connections. With that in mind, here are some questions for you to ask yourself ...

---

11 So many pandemic homeschooling parents are still traumatised by their first ever wet break scenario.

HOW WELCOMING AM I?

I know that you're busy, and pressed for time, and a bit stressed, and in need of a coffee – and so are many parents. However, a smile and a chat will go a long way to making your life easier in the long run. If school was a traumatic place for certain parents, a smile and a warm welcome can help break down barriers and change perceptions.

Beyond the welcome outside of the classroom, are you finding opportunities to ensure that parents step into and then spend time in your classroom? There are many formal opportunities for school visits, which may scare some parents, but inviting them in ten minutes before school starts or before home time to see a gallery of work, for example, is powerful.

Remember, it's not all about the learning. Make a human connection. Enquire about how they are, wish them a good day, ask how their day was, ask what they're doing at the weekend or what their plans for the holiday are. Ensure that they know you care about their child and their child's family. Building these relationships one natter at a time may not directly improve the learning but will go a long way to improving your subsequent conversations and communication about the learning.

AM I PUTTING IN THE TIME AND EFFORT TO BUILD THIS RELATIONSHIP?

Be prepared for the fact that establishing a connection will not happen immediately. There may be some who will want to be on first-name terms and speak to you like an old friend within days, while others will take longer. That's why you persevere. I once had a parent ask me, not in the most welcoming of tones, 'Why do you always smile and ask us if we've had a good day?' When I explained that I saw our class as one extended family, which all parents were part of, she softened. Slightly. But I didn't give up and when she accompanied us on a school trip later in the year, she stated how much she loved watching the bond between the children in 'our' class. She also shared with me how she'd hated school, had effectively left at 14 and had never had a teacher take an interest in her, so had found being spoken to 'weird', especially as her child was in my Year 6 class and it had never happened before. You never know what they've been through or the baggage they bring with them along with their children each morning.

ARE YOU MAINTAINING YOUR NON-NEGOTIABLES AND BEING CONSISTENT WITH YOUR EXPECTATIONS?

I outlined the importance of these back in Chapter 1. While you might try to be accommodating of parents for the sake of your relationship with them, parents will, as sure as eggs is eggs, try to push boundaries.[12] So remember your non-negotiables. If necessary, get help from your year partner, key stage leader or even the SLT. They can be strategically stationed on the playground to head these parents off at the pass as and when needed.

In trying to build a positive, professional relationship in the best interests of the child, don't allow your expectations to slip. After all, like a kayak in the middle aisle of Aldi, once they're gone, they're gone. Despite your friendliness, ultimately, you are there to be their child's teacher, not their friend, and the child's learning and your professionalism should always come first.

---

12 The parent who thinks drop-off and pick-up is all about them and their child, regardless of how many other parents want – or need – a chat, I'm looking at you.

ARE YOU SHARING?

With all the various technological means we have at our disposal, there is no excuse for not sharing ideas, learning and prompts with parents. For example, a private class Twitter account that only parents are allowed to follow makes it very easy for teachers to communicate directly with home. Share examples of work or the models you are using in class that they can also use at home. What about sharing videos of activities or the children explaining the games they are playing? Or talking about the day when a special guest came to visit, especially if this involved parents signing up and making a contribution? Twitter limits the length of the videos you upload, which is quite helpful and keeps you focused, but other platforms let you have longer to show what has been happening. Another idea is to share prompts for discussions that you have had in class that can also be explored at home. For example, 'Today we discussed whether Henry VIII was a good king or not, so ask your child what they think tonight. They should be able to give you points for both sides of the argument.'

Never underestimate the ability of children to neglect to tell their parents all the good stuff that happened that day, or fail to magnify the tiniest argument, comment or problem into a trauma of epic proportions.[13] Therefore, as a child leaves, a quick 'Make sure you tell your mum/dad about ...' is really powerful, as is taking work out with you to share at the gate (on a dry day). The first time you do this, perhaps the reaction will be cool, but persevere. It will be worth it.

A personal favourite of mine is to announce, in a grave tone, to a parent that you were forced to send their child to the head teacher, before you break into a smile and

---

13 Creasy's Third Law of Parental Dynamics: for every child's action, there will be an equal and opposite parental overreaction.

explain that it was for an excellent piece of work or behaviour. This is even better if the child plays along, especially if – as was the case with Joe in my class over ten years ago – the child is infamous for being sent to the head for all the wrong reasons. His performance was worthy of an Oscar and the look on his mum's face – not to mention the other parents' – was priceless.

HOW DO YOU SHARE THE NEGATIVES?

A simple maxim has stood me in good stead here over the years: praise in public; criticise in private.

If there is the need to have a negative conversation with a parent, then make sure you do this away from the curious ears and judging eyes of the playground. If possible, get someone else in to dismiss your class while you speak to the parent early, taking them into a quiet space inside the school, not the playground. Remember to be clear and concise too.

A teacher challenging the behaviour of their child or reporting an incident in which their child played a role is never easy for any parent to hear, but is best done in private, with the events and outcomes clearly and concisely described. Ensure you allow for any questions and, if you don't know or need to get back to them, say so and make sure that you do.

Despite all your best efforts, there may be the need to have a conversation that you'd rather not have about any number of things:

- Lack of or incomplete PE kit.
- Not reading at home.
- Not completing home learning.

- The child coming in tired (and telling you they had a late bedtime).

- Lack of lunch/snack or water bottle.

- Bringing in a banned snack (e.g. chocolate).

- Inappropriate language.

These are just a few of the topics that I have had to bring up in 'that conversation' with parents and, although they may seem trivial, they aren't as they all relate to the child's well-being and learning. The same mantra holds true: the conversation needs to be had in private and your concerns should be expressed clearly and in a non-judgemental manner. Explaining, as I once heard a colleague do, that you know this is an issue because it was the same last year with the child's older sibling is sending a clear message that the parent is the one at fault. This may be true, but it's neither helpful nor constructive.

It's also important that you have any difficult conversations you need to have sooner rather than later. 'Eat that frog' as the saying goes.[14] This approach also applies to emails. If you receive an email that warrants a delicate or tricky response, reply sooner rather than later, as the volatility of the parents may well rise if they perceive that you are making them wait for no other reason than because you want to.

Ensure that details of these conversations and/or emails are passed onwards and upwards. Not only will they contribute to a bigger picture, which is especially important if there are any potential safeguarding issues, but they also protect you should a parent raise any issues in future. It

---

14 Mark Twain allegedly said, but probably didn't, 'If it's your job to eat a frog, it's best to do it first thing in the morning. If it's your job to eat two frogs, eat the biggest one first.' This advice holds true regardless. Get the unpleasant thing done sooner rather than later.

also allows you to have full notes and information ready for your end-of-year handover. I find using a spreadsheet for the class, in which you keep a record of everything, is helpful and can be easily passed on to the receiving teacher.

DO YOU REMEMBER THAT BOUNDARIES ARE IMPORTANT?

This is not only with regards to the drop-off and collection, but emails as well. I recommend that you make sure there is a clear delineation between your work time and personal time. Some parents will expect an immediate response to their emails, irrespective of the time of day. This boundary needs to be addressed early and clearly, and then maintained. How you do this is up to you, but the following tips may help:

- Create an automated out-of-office response explaining that during the day you are teaching and in the evenings you will not be monitoring work emails, but you will respond when you can.

- Make your expectations clear. For example, don't check emails during teaching hours and definitely don't respond to them. I have found that a simple but effective way to handle emails is to check them before and after school and, if I have time, at lunch. I will respond to them then.

If I receive an email during the evening, I may well see it, but (depending on the urgency of the content) will probably not respond until the morning. I probably can't deal with the issue from home anyway. An automated response takes the pressure off, as does a quick 'Thank you for your email. Unfortunately I cannot deal with it now, but tomorrow I will ... and then will get back to you by ...', which often works wonders with parents. This is especially true for those who are venting (as we all do from time to time), who are surprised that you have taken family time to respond. I've even had parents apologise for interrupting my evening.

Few emails sent outside of working hours are genuinely urgent (apart from the ones that genuinely are) and that includes any from your head teacher. Often, when they are sent says more about when it suited the sender, and they don't expect you to respond immediately.[15]

SHOWS AND PERFORMANCES

In the same way that some teachers can be frustrated artists whose only creative outlet is the display board, others are unfulfilled West End directors (or worse, performers) whose time comes with the culmination of the school year: the school show.

Of course, such events are important for adults and children alike, creating memories that endure as the memory of what a fronted adverbial is or why anyone needs to know in the first place fades. Like spelling tests and cheap black plimsoles, they are a primary school rite of passage and need to be treated as such. The secret is to achieve this in a way that doesn't lead to a nervous breakdown for the teachers concerned.

For Year 6, the school show marks the end of their primary schooling. For other year groups, the nativity, carol concert or other Christmas event will be the creative highlight of the year. Depending on your school, there may be other

---

15 A standard footer on an email along the lines of 'I don't expect a response outside of normal working hours, although I am happy to receive one' is always welcome.

big events, including special assemblies, all of which will also serve the purpose of getting the parents in.

Regardless of your school's performance calendar, here are some suggestions to help you work smarter and avoid gin and tears before bedtime:

- It's a school show, not a Broadway production. A few missed lines are fine. People expect it and it adds to the fun.

- Remember, only you and the children know exactly what's in the script, what should be being said, by whom and when. So, if a few lines are missed, or said in the wrong order, or not recited exactly as per the script, don't stress it – go with it. I've seen some children create amazing ad-libs that bring on raucous laughter from the audience, so relax and go with the flow.

- Involve the children – let them choose the show. They will have more investment in it that way. Similarly, if it's a termly performance, such as an assembly or an end-of-unit show-and-tell with your class, let them write their own lines. Again, the investment levels will rise, and they are more likely to remember their lines too.

- Be prepared to discover star talent you didn't know you had, such as the child who has listened to read-throughs and memorised the entire script.[16] You might discover who the natural performer is in your class (not to be confused with the class show-off), who can rescue a scene when there is a momentary lapse of concentration by the third shepherd who has just spotted his nan in the audience.

---

16 Such children – and my daughter was one – make great prompts and are worth their weight in gold as stand-ins too.

- Start early – don't make it a last-minute rush. Working on a performance is a great learning break.

- Songs are your responsibility; learning the lines is theirs! This is something to ensure you share with parents in the weeks leading up to the performance via social media and in person.

- Set a clear deadline for when you'll be rehearsing without scripts. And stick to it – for everyone – however painful.

- Check who needs support and make sure they get it.

- Don't over-rehearse. You don't need to run through the whole thing *every* time.

- Cast carefully. Use the funny child for the funny part, the loud voice for the narrator, and so on.

- Encourage the children to support each other. Those who can remember the lines should work with those who can't or, if someone only has a few lines or isn't performing, they can help the children with larger parts memorise their lines.

- Not everyone will want to perform all the time. Give the children the choice.[17] And do this without the parents having input. They might want their child to have the main role, but the child might not agree!

- Be prepared for absentees. It will happen, just when you fear it most.

- Make the children responsible for their own rehearsals and get them to work on their scenes together. I once saw a group playing football and calling out their lines to each other as they passed the ball.

---

17 But everyone joins in the singing.

- Have a few shows each time so that all parents can attend. This means a daytime performance as well as the more traditional after-school one. This allows younger children who are not yet school age to attend too.

- Talking of which, invite the youngest children to a full rehearsal. A word of caution, though. They are unlikely to get all the jokes, so make sure you have primed the staff to laugh at the right times, otherwise it puts your class off. Here speaks the voice of experience.

- Don't interrupt a dress rehearsal in front of an audience. Follow up on any issues later. It's better for the children's confidence that way.

- Call on other suitable adults or older children to help you – for example, backstage with costume changes, music or lighting, or front of house roles. Don't try to do it all yourself.

- Throughout the performance, whatever goes wrong, smile. Then, during the final song, it's perfectly permissible to cry.

And remember, it's supposed to be an enjoyable event for you and the children. Make sure it is.

CHAPTER CONTEMPLATIONS

I have covered a variety of topics in this final chapter, but I think you will still spot a common thread: the importance of your professional integrity (not to mention your sanity).

Therefore, when considering any of the aspects covered in this chapter, ask yourself these simple questions:

● Why am I doing this?

● Where are the children in all of this?

● Whether I am considering display boards, parental engagement or shows, how can I improve things progressively and systematically?

And, for me, the most important consideration of all:

● Is the effort I put in going to give me at least an equal or, preferably greater, return in terms of output? Never mistake being busy for being effective or treat being tired as evidence that you're doing the right thing. Being the last one to leave each day is not proof that you care more than your colleagues do. Fatigue is not a competitive sport.

FINAL THOUGHTS

And that's all there is to it.

Hopefully throughout this book you've found things to challenge, question and inspire you. I hope you are reassured to see that you are following some of this advice already and have encountered plenty of ideas you hadn't thought of but are going to take out for a spin and approaches that you want to think about some more. Not to mention the ideas that you once tried that didn't work but that you want to have another stab at now.

Essentially, this book is about the one thing that all teaching is about: love. It may sound a little schmaltzy but it's true (and check out the work of the aforementioned Dr Andrew Curran for more on the link between love and childhood brain development). It's true whether you work in the primary, secondary or tertiary phase, or in special needs or alternative provision, or any other variation on a theme when it comes to helping children be all they can be and all they can become.

Love.

I love my job. I decided that I wanted to be a teacher when I was eight and I haven't regretted choosing it as my career, despite the hurdles and challenges I have faced during my time in the classroom, even when they seemed insurmountable.

I love the children I work with – I tell them this often and my favourite class is *always* the one I'm currently teaching.

I love learning – I think this is the essence of being a teacher. You need to be the best learner too.

I love trying to help others – hence this book and my work with Independent Thinking, speaking to educators and school leaders around the country.[1]

There are many differences between myself and all my various Independent Thinking colleagues, but there is at least one thing that unites us. The belief that, when it comes to teaching and learning, there is always another way.

---

1 If I can be of further help, or you want to discuss any of my approaches or ideas, feel free to get in touch via Twitter. I'm @EP3577. If you know me, you'll know why that's my handle.

APPENDIX 1: HOME LEARNING EXEMPLAR

This example is for Year 5 home learning for the autumn term.

DAILY TASKS

READING

Aim for variety: books, magazines, newspapers, the internet, picture books, comics, recipe books, atlases, signs, etc.

- Read every day for at least ten minutes.

- Children should be heard reading at least three times a week.

- Children should hear an adult read at least three times a week.

MATHS

Times tables: focus on fluency in all tables – up to 12 x 12. Times Tables Rock Stars is perfect for this.

Decimals: as we are looking at this topic, going shopping and being aware of money will really help.

Place value: practise reading and writing large numbers (up to seven digits) in both numerals and words.

Time: practise reading analogue clocks as well as knowing how long until and since an event.

EVERYDAY LEARNING

Discuss the news, the weather, their interests, your day – whatever it is, don't underestimate the power of talking, without devices or distractions.

Playing board games and cards is a great way to have conversations with less pressure, as is going for a walk together, spotting the natural world around us.

EXTENSION ACTIVITIES – THE TUDORS

Building on our theme, ask your child to select two activities from the table to complete by half-term.

Whatever your child chooses should reflect their efforts and be their own work – make sure they take pride in whatever they do!

Imagine that you are going to meet Henry VIII. Design an outfit to wear – it needs to be Tudor clothing, not modern!	Research: ● A famous Tudor person. ● Tudor sport (you know about bear baiting already). ● How people lived. ● A choice of your own.	Create your own activity.
Draw a picture of a famous Tudor building (e.g. Windsor Castle, the Globe Theatre, Deal Castle).	The Tudors	Imagine that you are going to host a banquet for Henry VIII, write a menu 'fit for a king'. You may want to research the foods that Tudors ate.
Make and label a model of a famous Tudor building using recycled materials (e.g. cereal boxes, paper, toilet rolls, foil trays, etc.).	Use your knowledge of the Tudors and create a family tree for them. You can present this in any way you wish – be creative!	Imagine that you are going to meet Henry VIII. Write a diary entry for your day, including lots of feelings and descriptions.

APPENDIX 2: WORKING SMARTER TRANSITION DOCUMENT

Your school will undoubtedly have its own pro forma, but, in my experience, these are cumbersome and don't tend to tell you what you want and need to know. Here's a template for a simplified document that I always use – usually completed by me, during or after discussions and observations.

Name:	
Home life:	
Areas of strength:	
Ways to support their learning:	
Highlights of their year:	
Three words to describe them:	

You'll undoubtedly have noticed that this is all about the positive aspects of the learner – I can work the rest out for myself, or I'll have already heard talk in meetings or the staffroom. This document is to help my teaching and their learning, not for character assassination!

The home life section is vital. It's amazing how frequently colleagues can forget the impact this has on a child – for example, where are they in the sibling order? Are their parents separated (and, if so, what are the living arrangements/frequency of visits)? Are they a young carer? Sometimes, inadvertently, colleagues forget this information as they 'thought everyone knew', so I make a point of asking.

APPENDIX 3: MINUTES EXEMPLAR

Minutes for: [meeting date]

Present	
Apologies	
Absent	

Agenda item	Discussion	Decision	Action

LIST OF WORKING SMARTER TIPS

CHAPTER 1: DAILY ROUTINES

Make everyone accountable 10

Give real responsibilities 11

Think before you speak 15

Make sure the learning doesn't stop when it pauses 16

'Fail to prepare, prepare to fail' 19

Do you see what they see? 22

Meet them and greet them 22

Make the parent drop-off work for you 24

Start as you mean to go on 27

Never be afraid of the different or quirky 30

Surviving assemblies 33

Getting attention easily, without the burden 42

Handing out letters 47

CHAPTER 2: IN THE CLASSROOM

Make the most of planning, preparation and assessment
(PPA) time 54

Let cross-curricular learning help your planning 57

Plan for every child 61

Use online resources sparingly 66

Read the research 71

Who is the marking for? 72

Change the learner, not the work 72

Make the most of what you already do 74

Make learning fun! 77

CHAPTER 3: LEARNING OUTSIDE THE CLASSROOM

Get the children out promptly 84

Carry work over to after playtime 85

Walk with a purpose 86

Play with the children 86

Eat with the children 92

Vary who you sit with 94

Help out 94

Be in your room sometimes 95

Know the school's expectations 99

Model the work 100

Use technology to help you 101

Make use of early morning work 103

Support parents effectively 104

Remember lockdown 108

CHAPTER 4: TESTING

Know your curriculum 112

Test first 112

Call it what it is but don't make it a big deal 113

'Failure' is OK 114

Prepare for tests 115

It's not all about the scores 116

Not all tests are created equal 116

Make marking easy 117

Don't stress 'em, embrace 'em 120

Recognise that language counts 127

Familiarity doesn't need to breed contempt 128

Don't make it your force majeure 128

Remember what the test tests 129

Read, read, read 129

CHAPTER 5: TRANSITION

Make them feel special, regardless 142

Never make light of the change 143

Start before the start 144

Talk isn't cheap 145

Find out what works 145

Know what works, then be prepared to challenge or
change it 146

Really start on transition day 148

Know who they are 150

Step up incrementally 151

Remember that a rising tide raises all ships 152

It's not all about SATs/entrance exams/end-of-key-stage
tests 153

The early bird catches the worm 154

CHAPTER 6: WORKING WITH ADULTS

Above all else, the site manager is king 164

The office staff are queens 165

The cleaners are part of the extended royal family 167

First plan together, then plan separately 168

Make sure you share resources 169

Make time to share strategies 169

Be prepared to discuss your classes honestly 170

Make time to care for each other too 171

Don't deliberately exclude anyone 172

Variety is the spice of life 172

Triangles are strong structures 173

Remember that knowledge is power 180

Empower, don't disempower 181

Recognise them as part of the team 182

Know what you want from leaders 184

Know who does what 186

Know how they communicate (and what they mean) 186

Ask the SLT what, why and how 187

Meet deadlines 188

Seek advice 189

For better as well as for worse 190

Remember that the SLT are people too 191

CHAPTER 7: A MISCELLANY OF SMART WAYS OF WORKING

Ask yourself what your presentation says about you 201

REFERENCES AND FURTHER READING

Collin, J. and Quigley, A. (2021) *Teacher Feedback to Improve Pupil Learning: Guidance Report* (London: Education Endowment Foundation). Available at: https://educationendowmentfoundation.org.uk/education-evidence/guidance-reports/feedback#nav-download-the-guidance-report-and-poster.

Creasy, M. (2014) *Unhomework: How to Get the Most out of Homework without Really Setting It* (Carmarthen: Independent Thinking Press).

Curran, A. (2008) *The Little Book of Big Stuff About the Brain: The True Story of Your Amazing Brain* (Carmarthen: Crown House Publishing).

Elliot, V., Baird, J., Hopfenbeck, T. N., Ingram, J., Thompson, I., Usher, N., Zantout, M., Richardson, J. and Coleman, R. (2016) *A Marked Improvement? A Review of the Evidence on Written Marking* (London: Education Endowment Foundation). Available at: https://educationendowmentfoundation.org.uk/education-evidence/evidence-reviews/written-marking.

Gilbert, I. (2007) *The Little Book of Thunks: 260 Questions to Make Your Brain Go Ouch!* (Carmarthen: Crown House Publishing).

Gilbert, I. (2017) *The Compleat Thunks Book* (Carmarthen: Independent Thinking Press).

Jackson, N. (2009) *The Little Book of Music in the Classroom: Using Music to Improve Memory, Motivation, Learning and Creativity* (Carmarthen: Crown House Publishing).

Lear, J. (2015) *Guerrilla Teaching: Revolutionary Tactics for Teachers on the Ground, in Real Classrooms, Working with Real Children, Trying to Make a Real Difference* (Carmarthen: Independent Thinking Press).

McFall, M. (2013) *The Little Book of Awe and Wonder: A Cabinet of Curiosities* (Carmarthen: Independent Thinking Press).

Martin, R. A. (n.d.) Do Children Laugh Much More Often Than Adults Do? *Association for Applied and Therapeutic Humor*. Available at: https://aath.memberclicks.net/do-children-laugh-much-more-often-than-adults-do.

Ofsted (2021) *School Inspection Handbook* (1 October). Available at: https://www.gov.uk/government/publications/school-inspection-handbook-eif.

Peat, J. (2018) Only 30% of Parents Read Stories to Their Children Every Day, Poll Claims, *The Independent* (31 August). Available at: https://www.independent.co.uk/life-style/health-and-families/parents-reading-children-books-uk-roald-dahl-mcdonalds-damian-hinds-a8516436.html?r=35964.

Robertson, J. (2014) *Dirty Teaching: A Beginner's Guide to Learning Outdoors* (Carmarthen: Independent Thinking Press).

Seuss, Dr. (1960) *One Fish, Two Fish, Red Fish, Blue Fish* (New York: Random House).

Shibli, D. and West, R. (2018) Cognitive Load Theory and Its Application in the Classroom, *Impact: Journal of the Chartered College of Teaching* (February). Available at: https://impact.chartered.college/article/shibli-cognitive-load-theory-classroom/.

Smith, J. (2017) *The Lazy Teacher's Handbook: How Your Students Learn More When You Teach Less*, new edn (Carmarthen: Independent Thinking Press).

978-178135337-0

978-178135338-7

978-178135339-4

978-178135340-0

978-178135341-7

978-178135369-1

978-178135373-8

978-178135400-1

978-178135353-0

ındependent thinking press ☙

www.independentthinkingpress.com

independent thinking

Independent Thinking. An education company.

Taking people's brains for a walk since 1994.

We use our words.

www.independentthinking.com